"For years, I have howled in laughter, nodded in agreement, and marveled in wonder at the wit and wisdom that Meghan Leahy has offered parents as a parent educator and writer for *The Washington Post*. In *Parenting Outside the Lines*, Meghan shares a deep dive into her thinking, offering parents of all ages not only guidance on how to handle the inevitable challenges of parenting, whether for tots or teens, but more importantly a "true north" of connection to guide us when we invariably find ourselves in the unchartered terrain that defines modern parenting. A gift to parents, whether to yourself or others, this is a book to learn from, laugh at, and live with, helping you be the parent Meghan confidently assures you already resides within you."

—Ned Johnson, coauthor of *The Self-Driven Child*

"Meghan Leahy's book *Parenting Outside the Lines* reads like a reassuring chat with your older, wiser sister, helping pare away the anxiety that can surround parenting today. Leahy's deep appreciation for the challenging process of growing a human shines through the no-nonsense writing. With wisdom won through years of working with families, she helps readers understand how they may be sabotaging happy family life. Packed with common sense and road-tested ideas, *Parenting Outside the Lines* is the insightful, compassionate book that today's parents need to raise their children more confidently and joyfully."

—Katherine Reynolds Lewis,
author of *The Good News About Bad Behavior*

"A book for every parent who needs the courage, guidance, and kick in the pants to stop what's not working and start over. Refreshingly honest and deeply wise, a blend of brain science and stand-up, this one's a lifesaver."

—Karen Maezen Miller,
author of *Momma Zen* and *Hand Wash Cold*

"Meghan Leahy claims to have written a parenting book free of data and studies, but she has actually written one that leans into some of the most important research of all: life experience. This book is equal parts humble and hilarious, deeply wise and immediately actionable. It's like a how-to book and a parenting memoir had a baby. Reading *Parenting Outside the Lines* is time well spent."

—Cara Natterson, MD, author of *Decoding Boys*

"The truth is, no one knows more about parenting our children than we do ourselves—but it's so hard to hear our own voices above the cacophony of information. Fortunately, no one knows more about helping parents learn to trust themselves than Meghan Leahy. You've always known you have the capacity to build a joyful family life. *Parenting Outside the Lines* will help you find it."

—KJ Dell'Antonia, author of *How to Be a Happier Parent*

Parenting
Outside
the Lines

Parenting Outside the Lines

Forget the Rules, Tap into Your Wisdom,
and Connect with Your Child

Meghan Leahy

A TarcherPerigee Book

tarcherperigee

an imprint of Penguin Random House LLC
penguinrandomhouse.com

The author acknowledges permission to reprint the following: "Things You Didn't Put on Your Résumé." Reprinted from *Carrying Water to the Field: New and Selected Poems* by Joyce Sutphen by permission of the University of Nebraska Press. Copyright 2019 by the Board of Regents of the University of Nebraska.

Most TarcherPerigee books are available at special quantity discounts for bulk purchase for sales promotions, premiums, fund-raising, and educational needs. Special books or book excerpts also can be created to fit specific needs. For details, write: SpecialMarkets@penguinrandomhouse.com.

Library of Congress Cataloging-in-Publication Data

Names: Leahy, Meghan, author.
Title: Parenting outside the lines: forget the rules, tap into your wisdom, and connect with your child / Meghan Leahy.
Description: New York: TarcherPerigee, an imprint of Penguin Random House LLC, 2020
Identifiers: LCCN 2020000675 (print) | LCCN 2020000676 (ebook) | ISBN 9780525541219 (hardcover) | ISBN 9780525541226 (ebook)
Subjects: LCSH: Parenting. | Child rearing.
Classification: LCC HQ755.8 .L3747 2020 (print) | LCC HQ755.8 (ebook) | DDC 649/.1—dc23
LC record available at https://lccn.loc.gov/2020000675
LC ebook record available at https://lccn.loc.gov/2020000676
p.   cm.

Printed in the United States of America
10   9   8   7   6   5   4   3   2   1

Book design by Elke Sigal

For Mark, who believed in me from the start

For my loves, Gigi, Louise, and Sophia,
for eating my salmon dinners

CONTENTS

I would like to beg you, dear Sir, as well as I can, to have patience with everything unresolved in your heart and to try to love the questions themselves as if they were locked rooms or books written in a very foreign language. Don't search for the answers, which could not be given to you now, because you would not be able to live them. And the point is, to live everything. Live the questions now. Perhaps then, someday far in the future, you will gradually, without even noticing it, live your way into the answer.

—RAINER MARIA RILKE, *Letters to a Young Poet*

"Parenting outside the lines." What does that even mean and what "lines" am I referring to? In my mind, these lines are all the parenting "rules" that have been torturing you, me, *all* parents, for time immemorial. These parenting lines and rules and boxes are both prisons of our own making as well as ideals that our culture keeps perpetuating to keep us in a chronic tizzy. We resent being told how to raise our kids, being told what is right and what is wrong, yet we cannot stand the ambiguity, doubt, and uncertainty that comes with raising our children; we cannot stand the feeling of being left in the dark. We don't just want a flashlight when it comes to our parenting worries, we want NFL stadium lighting; and when the lighting fails to show us the way, we blame the lights, ourselves, the kids, the spouse, society, the dog . . . you name it.

It is all very human to want answers to our parenting worries. Our brains are sense-making organs, constantly taking in the world and shuffling multiple pieces of information around. Here's my head on an average day:

Panic! I cannot find my keys! Wait, they are here in my hand!

I need to help my child with math and stir the soup before it burns.

Is every child already on Snapchat? Maybe my child games too much? How do other parents keep their kids off the iPad?

All of this is happening while I am getting ready for work. But as our brains clarify our immediate needs and keep us safe, it is easy to forget a couple of important parenting truths: First, we are *not* limited by the parenting lines that we (and society) have drawn, nor are we limited by our panicky brains. Second, we have the power to see the larger picture of our parenting lives and, third, connecting to our children trumps any other physical or emotional parenting need you can imagine.

As you read this book, I will be asking (challenging) you to break out of your self-imposed parenting prisons. I will ask you to embrace ambiguity and fear, become comfortable not knowing the answers, drop the to-do lists as well as the pursuit to find the "one way to be a good parent." Instead, we will befriend openness, curiosity, humility, and the wide-eyed wonder that parenting inevitably delivers on a regular basis. And in order to help you embrace this wide-eyed wonder, every chapter ends with a list of questions to consider. This is homework, yes, but not the kind of parenting homework to which you may be accustomed. I find that most parenting books are, in one way or another, trying to fix a problem (re: the child), and while that can be useful, that is not the purpose of the questions in this particular book. These questions (found at the conclusion of each chapter) are meant to draw you into a deeper understanding of yourself and your child. This understanding may lead to more thoughtfulness, and that may lead to even more questions. Think of it like a "Choose Your Own Adventure" parenting book, rather than a "How-To" parenting book. You may feel angry, annoyed, ambivalent, avoidant, or affronted by the questions, or you may feel cracked-open, clearheaded, curious, and freed by them. Whatever the feeling, I believe almost every movement toward understanding yourself is a move in the right direction. The questions in this book may not yield immediate results (they may tip the first domino of action) or they may lead to overnight changes; I don't know what will happen. I just know that these parenting questions are worth reading, pondering, and (hopefully) journaling out some insights.

Does embracing wide-eyed wonder about your parenting life sound like a load of BS? Maybe. I am guessing you have picked up this book because you are suffering. When it comes to your children, you are lost, unsure, sad, worried, and anxious. You are angry, frustrated, and sick of banging your head against the proverbial wall, and now, it doesn't sound like I am going to give you the answers. And we parents all want answers. You and I don't want wide-eyed wonder; we want our children to listen to us more and sass us less. So, why would I write a book that challenges you to ask yourself questions instead of giving you every answer for how to fix your children?

When I began my own family in 2004, some of my strongest memories are of me, lying pregnant in bed, reading book after book about parenting and child development. The books fell into two main categories: stages of child development or parent humor. I distinctly remember reading *The Girlfriends' Guide to Pregnancy* by Vicki Iovine, munching on saltine crackers and giggling endlessly. Because my anxiety kept me in a state of endless worry as well as that niggly feeling of "there is always something else to learn," a simple and funny parenting book was a breath of fresh air. While I loved (and still love) my development and theory books and they offered some wonderful clarity, they never really *fixed* anything. The more that the parenting books aimed to provide "the answer," the more limiting they felt to me (and most other parents I know, too). There were too many boxes to tick, too many of my protestations of "what about this or that," and I always found too many exceptions to the rules; it was crazy-making and I had hardly even begun the parenting journey myself!

For this book, I wondered: *Could I provide thoughtful questions? Could I write a book that helps you feel sane? Could I write a book that provides some hope, while also challenging you to be more compassionate, more loving, and more open to your child and yourself? Is there a way I can help you trust yourself? Help you recognize that you do have parenting intuition? Recognize that feeling unsure is not failure, rather it is proof you are on the right path and, finally, can we do all this and laugh a bit, too?* Let's lift the limits and the "shoulds" and "should nots" and find our own way through this parenting life. While quick fixes and bullet lists are tempting, maybe we can accept that our greatest parenting strengths rest in asking ourselves thoughtful questions and seeing where those answers take us. Our children are unique, and so our parenting of them is naturally customized (an idea that our larger culture doesn't seem to support). When we trust ourselves, we can (mostly) free ourselves from the fears that keep us panicked, reactionary, and disconnected from our children. That makes all the difference.

You *do* have parenting intuition.

As I kicked these ideas around, the first thing that had to go were all the data and studies that clutter up so many parenting books. Why? First, I didn't want the book to be so specifically tied to *this* date and time. My desire is that someone can pick up this book twenty years from now and still find the concepts useful and true (yeah, the tech stuff will be totally different, but hopefully the main ideas will still track). Second, we parents have never had so much information at our fingertips. There are checklists and articles and studies for every single parenting and family topic you can think of, and those articles and studies? They can often feel like they are saving your life! Parents who previously felt left in the dark and lonely now have entire communities at their fingertips. Stuck on how to get your ADHD kiddo to eat breakfast? There are entire websites, chock-full of data and studies, geared just toward this predicament! And that is awesome. But even though I love data and studies and internet support, I started noticing something interesting over the past couple of years in my parent coaching life.

The more I coached parents, the more I found that the studies and data and articles weren't really helping them. I mean, sure, it was interesting and I was always glad I had the research for my clients, but I found that the parents I worked with weren't suffering from a lack of information; they were suffering from a lack of self-awareness, trust in themselves, and loving connection with their children. They felt boxed in and limited, yet simultaneously untethered and adrift. I would say parents suffered from a lack of intuition, but it was more a lack of *listening* to that intuition. Because we have so much information at our fingertips and because so much of that information is contradictory (I mean, just look at sleep training . . . there are literally a million different ways to sleep train your child and to some extent, they are mostly all true), parents feel lost. And because I am seen as an "expert," I was inadvertently causing more stress to these parents by providing more studies, data, and research. The more I coached using studies, the more I could see how I was contributing to the very problem that brought the parents to me in the first place! Instead, as I decided to pivot toward coaching and coaxing out the intuition and common sense that was buried deep in every parent, a couple of questions emerged:

First, where *is* parental intuition nowadays? Is there such a thing? Was there ever such a thing? American parenting culture is new (relatively speaking), so we don't have a long history to draw from when it comes to modern parenting. We are, quite literally, making it up as we go along and, as scary as parenting in the twenty-first century can feel, I believe parents have felt lost, unsure, and unprepared for time eternal. And that is good! What if the common sense we so badly want *comes* out of feeling lost? What if the parenting path forward *only* becomes illuminated when we are stumbling in the dark?

Second, where are our parental hearts right now? Meaning, do we feel our way through our parenting lives at all, or is it only cerebral and thought-based and research-driven? The internet is an undeniable gift to most of us, but it also brings heaps of data that can prove to be more confusing than helpful. We search and search for answers for our parenting challenges, but in these endless searches, we are actually drawn further and further away from our hearts and emotions, as well as being drawn away from the actual child in front of us. It becomes so easy to lose sight of our parenting heart, our compassion, our gut, our trust that we know the way. Do we know our children with a truly open and trusting heart? Can we trust our emotions so that when we access the parenting data, it can ring more clearly true (or false, as the case may be)?

When I reflected on these questions, I immediately knew that I wanted to write a book to us, the parents who are afraid of not knowing what to *do*. The parents who want every answer in a trend or a bullet list (oh, how I love a bullet list), a theory or a strategy. The parents who have forgotten their intuition. I am writing this book as a path back to your heart when it comes to common, everyday parenting issues.

What Is My Background and How Did I Get Here? (Or Why Should You Listen to Me?)

I began my career, right out of college, as an English teacher for boys, sixth through twelfth grade. I then attended grad school to become a school counselor, quickly realized that I pretty much hated that job (never got to see the kids and always had to sit through the dullest of meetings with adults . . . yuck), then I had my own kids, became a volunteer parent educator, then became a certified parent coach, then started writing for the *Washington Post*, then met Dr. Gordon Neufeld and fell in love with his approach, then kept coaching and writing until poof! Here I am! Not one single decision in my life has been made knowing that I would be here. I mean, parent coaching? What kind of profession is that, anyway? And to tell you the truth, it *is* a pretty made-up job. I don't personally have any qualms about my work nor do I doubt that I help people, but let's face it: It sounds pretty ridiculous. Do we *really* need parent coaches in this day and age? I guess we do . . . but why? How did we get here?

I chalk up my profession to the happy and complicated confluence of women's liberation in the United States, how so many of us live emotionally as well as physically separated from our families of origin, and live separated from our neighbors and communities. (Don't worry, I am not dogging the modern American woman's life; to the contrary, there is no direction but forward for total equality for women. Anything else is unacceptable. And I don't think we all need to move directly next to our parents as adult children.) And yes, I know that our current parenting lives are complicated for a million reasons; I am just writing about what I have seen in my coaching experience.

For almost as long as women have walked the earth, women have been (with some exceptions) largely at home, tending to the immediate needs of the property and children.* And since women had almost no choice when it came to when and who they coupled with, as well as if and when and how many children they wanted to bear, there was very little discussion about how one should raise their families. You know how parents are free-range or helicopter or tech-free or family-bed-sharing now? Yeah, that was not the case for most humans walking the earth until fairly recently. Each family took on the larger culture, religion, and mores surrounding them, no questions asked. This made for a simpler way to raise a family! Even though women had virtually no voice and children were largely seen and not all that heard, family life was simple, predictable, and the

---

* It is important to note that while non-white parents in the United States may have some shared family experiences with their European and white counterparts (men and fathers holding all of the power in a family structure; women and mothers assuming all control of household and family duties), the systemic racism and lack of movement up the social and economic ladder has also contributed (and still contributes) to stark differences between the two groups when it comes to families. To properly understand parenting in America is to investigate all families, such as Latino families, African American families, and Asian families, as well as the multitudes of subsets of each of those cultures. These family lives are as varied and as rich as any in the world, and I would never attempt to be a voice for all parents; that would be a disservice to all families. There is also the ever-growing group of same-sex families that share typical parenting issues and must undertake our culture's mistrust and judgment of their parenting lives as well. Every time I talk about families and parents in this book, I will be addressing the deep needs that all humans share and these needs (mostly) transcend race, culture, and sexual orientation, but I have no doubt that I will misstep, not consider, and be blind to issues that my life has afforded me to not witness and experience. Please know that I am sensitive to this and am doing my very best, while still humbly admitting that I am as flawed as the next person out there.

parents' (men's) power was absolute. Parents (fathers) knew best.*
Period.

Fast-forward to women gaining some power: power to become educated, power to work, power to vote, power to take birth control and have autonomy over their own bodies, power to leave a marriage, power to never marry, power to move away from extended family and their hometowns, and power to run their lives, and you find the fastest shift in family structures that may have ever happened to humans and community.

And so why do people call me? Why do good parents pick up books like this? I mean, think about how your grandmother (or great-grandmother) lived and parented. Think about the rights (not) afforded to her, about what the larger culture allowed or didn't allow in parenting. The differences can be striking, and are you parenting *anything* like that? True, you maybe aren't the *polar* opposite of your preceding generations (or maybe you are), but take technology! That alone has utterly changed our parenting landscape, even if you are still working the same farm or living in the same small town you grew up in. Our ever-increasing internet-connected life is changing the way we parent, like it or not. Parents call me because they are either not close to their extended family or they can no longer relate to their elders; *the people from whom they would traditionally take their parenting cues.* For better or worse, the way "things have always been done" is not working for the modern parent. And this requires new supports; people like me.

I see my role as a parenting coach as culling the immense wisdom, experience, and knowledge of the previous generations of parents,

---

* There are some notable women-led, matriarchal, and matrilineal cultures in the world, such as the Mosuo in the Himalayas, the Bribri in Costa Rica, and the Minangkabau in Indonesia. Peek at these cultures; fascinating stuff!

combining it with today's science and real-world parenting needs, and helping each and every parent find their intuitive voice. Because you see, we humans haven't changed all that much over the millions of years we have been parenting, and even though your parenting problems feel real and huge (and they are), the brain that is worrying right now about your child is just like the brain that worried one hundred, two hundred, five hundred years ago. Your parenting situation is utterly unique *and* completely ordinary. Cool, right?

My parenting-coach hope is that we all slow down a little, zoom out, see the needs of the situation, and not make haphazard and overly emotional or overly rational decisions . . . Is that too much to ask as a coach? It definitely is, but I am going for it, anyway.

What Do I Believe In? What's My Take? Which Parenting Trend Do I Support?

People ask me this a lot. Like, a lot a lot. And let's face it, you really want to know this before you dive into the book. I often answer that I just want parents to stop losing their goddamn minds. We all laugh, but then I keep standing there like, "No, really. That's what I want to happen." I am being facetious, but only a little.

I believe in Tiger Parenting because being a strong parent with a clear voice, a concise point of view, and unyielding boundaries teaches a child responsibility and respect. It is also the most depressing and, frankly, scary method of parenting I have ever seen. There is little fun and it seems like there are few chances for the child to express a need, want, or desire. I just don't know how the tiger parent ends up with an emotionally healthy adult, at least in the way we Americans understand emotional health (which could be up for debate).

I believe in Slow Parenting. And yes, in case you haven't heard of it, it's a real thing. It is when kids have very few structured activities and the freedom to explore the environment freely around them. And this sounds *awesome* in theory, if the parent doesn't have a job and also has endless patience to follow their child over hill and dale, smelling the roses, not to mention lives in or near a place that is safe to meander through and has fresh roses to smell. And meanwhile, who is making dinner and picking up the toys while there is all this to-ing and fro-ing? I don't know.

I believe in French Parenting, which has you speaking to your baby as if he were an adult, giving your children zero choices when it comes to food, starting them on cigs at five (I kid, I kid), and expecting them to have patience at all times. The only problem is, you know, that some kids have other emotional, physical, and learning needs . . . So, yeah, not sure what those Frenchies do about differently wired children, but c'est la vie. They also have *free* universal childcare in France, so it must be a little easier to be patient and teach patience when you have that kind of support, literally, on every corner. We American parents cannot even fathom this kind of support and *time*.

I believe in Free-Range Parenting because children are far more resourceful and responsible than we give them credit for. And while I would love every child to roam freely, many neighborhoods are simply not set up for children to wander around. Not to mention that, for many children, it really isn't safe. (I live in DC and many children cannot safely walk from home to school, let alone find a nice park or beautiful woods to explore.) Also the twenty-four-hour news cycle has us in a 24/7 panicked state regarding kidnap and assault, making it hard for us parents to just release our littles into the world. (Parents calling the cops on fellow parents is often a bigger threat than kidnappers, by the way.)

I believe in Helicopter Parenting because many of our children need far more attention than they are currently receiving (especially emotionally speaking). Many parents expect children to solve problems that are not developmentally appropriate and require more adult assistance, and so helicopter parents know that children need more support. But Helicopter Parenting, when a parent hovers over their children and chronically and constantly chirps in with their advice and instructions, also stifles a child's ability to cope with the basic day-to-day challenges in life. This trend often results in anxious and insecure children.

I believe in Lawnmower Parenting (which is when the parent removes every emotional problem or physical obstacle in the child's path) because it's our parenting job to not allow our children to suffer beyond the point of it being helpful. And we don't want our children to run into the same issue over and over, without any hope of learning or growing, especially if that child has a differently wired brain! But removing too many obstacles from our children's path leads our children to believe that they will never experience hardship or anguish, again leading our children down a future path of shock, lack of resilience, and anxiety. Like helicopter parents, lawnmower parents look like good caretakers, but are usually avoided by the other adults in the child's life. (They are *those* parents in school; the ones trying to control every aspect of the child's future life.)

I believe in Attachment Parenting (which is not the same as Attachment Theory) because all studies point to a child thriving when in close proximity to their parents. The younger the child, the greater the need to be closer to the parent (or caregiver). This close proximity helps a child's nervous system calm down, hence helping their brains grow and mature. But if taken too far, parents can become enmeshed with their children. Soon, the child is calling the shots for every decision in the family. Give too much power to an immature person, and you've got a spoiled kid who feels entitled. And a family bed? I dunno, I can barely share my bed with my spouse comfortably . . .

I believe in Positive Parenting because, hello? Who doesn't want to be positive? Who doesn't want to be patient, compassionate, and loving? And much of the Positive Parenting lingo is awesome, but if not used correctly it becomes too "talky," wishy-washy, and even developmentally inappropriate. (There are typical Positive Parenting techniques that prove disastrous for children with executive functioning issues.) I also bristle at the idea that everything in parenting needs to be painted with a positive brush; just that thought makes me roll my eyes. The tenets of Positive Parenting are strong, but a lazy interpretation of this theory puts the child too much in the driver's seat of the family and that, my friend, is a recipe for disaster.

I believe in Mindful Parenting because, like Positive Parenting, who doesn't want to be mindful? What parent doesn't want to be more aware of her own interior world? Her own triggers? And stop reacting, reacting, reacting? If anything, this book is most closely tied to the Mindful Parenting approach, except that I am not going to ask you to meditate (unless you want to) nor am I going to ask you to help your children be more mindful. In my mind, children don't need to become more mindful; they already *are* mindful. It is we parents who need to become more introspective, not our children. Mindful Parenting (also known as Conscious Parenting) has little catchphrases like this one: "Parent without fear." These types of statements irk me because, as long as you have a human brain, you live with fear. Should I tell my friend, whose child is suffering terribly from the side effects of cancer treatments, to not be fearful? Should I tell a client, whose child is being bullied terribly at school, to not be fearful? Should we look at the environment and not have fear for our children? No! Fear is an important emotion; I never, ever want a parent trading in their fear for some kind of blasé, meme-happy parenting trend. There are not enough eye rolls for how I feel about the wellness lifestyle inserting itself into parenting. So, yeah . . . that's how I feel about *that*.

Unless a parenting trend or theory espouses physically and emotionally harming and shaming children, I probably agree with some aspect of it. Every single trend has a nugget of truth in it.

Do children need to be outside more and exploring nature? Yes.

Do children need more supervision and support in certain areas? Yes.

Do children simply need to eat what they are served without being offered an array of choices? Yes (mostly).

Do children have too many activities? Yes and no. (Are we just talking about upwardly mobile families? Those kids likely have too many, but there are scads of communities where children desperately need more activities.)

Do children need to have more adults hovering over them? Yes!

Do children need more freedom to fail, learn, and move on? Yes.

Do children need stronger boundaries? Yes.

Do children need to be physically close to their parents? Yes.

Do children need compassionate communication? Yes.

Do children need adults to be awake and mindful? Yes.

Yes, yes, yes.

So, if you love one (or a couple) of these parenting trends and are unhappy that I just reduced it to a three-sentence paragraph, don't worry. I love these trends, too; there's nothing inherently wrong with them. The problem occurs when we parents blindly adopt these trends despite the mounting evidence that that trend ain't working for our kiddos. Finally, we can get so busy parenting according to a theory that we actually disconnect from our child: The child becomes more of a project than a person. And this is where we begin to typically overparent; we leave our intuition, and forget our parenting hearts. We begin to draw the parenting "lines" that I want us to avoid.

For instance . . .

When a "slow parent" hires me because she is an introvert (I get it) and has her kids in zero activities, but she happens to mother a ten-year-old child who is bouncing off of the walls, and said child is begging for an organized sport. Any sport. The mother doesn't want him to play anything: "too many practices," "too many obligations," "not good for children to be so busy." It is clear that the child has a motor in him that is dying to be run, trained, and be part of a team. But this trend, which has great ideas at the root of it, is resulting in a misbehaving, whining, and miserable child. The parenting trend doesn't fit the needs of the family.

Or take the example of my friend Abigail, who was raised by European parents and wanted to bring a no-nonsense parenting ideal into her parenting life. A combination of *Battle Hymn of the Tiger Mother* and *Bringing Up Bébé*, if you will. She was tough as hell, often loving, and created rules that seemed both premature and arbitrary. The real problem? Her daughter was the most sensitive, sweetest girl you have ever laid eyes on. She already *wanted* to be good for her mother. My friend didn't need to bark at her and create these arbitrary rules at every turn. This insistence to be a tough and unyielding mother only made her daughter an anxious mess, unsure of her own voice, and afraid to ask for what she needed in school and in her own life.

Or my client Leslie, who hated her authoritarian and rigid upbringing, so she decided to really attach *and* simultaneously let loose with her twins. She believed that her children would let her know exactly what they would need when they needed it, and that her job was simply to pay attention and attend. This worked beautifully when the children were babies, but soon they matured into willful four-year-olds and Leslie was being dragged around by the nose. Leslie found herself angry, resentful, and most of all confused. She was attaching like hell to these kids; why were they such nightmares?

Or my client Ramona and her spouse, Frank. They carefully and consciously decided to take a Positive Parenting approach to their children. Their eldest child, a six-year-old named Lila, was a "handful," as they put it. Every single time they said, "Lila, when you hit us, we feel sad," Lila would stick out her tongue and spit at her parents, "I DON'T CARE!" The parents would respond with, "It sounds, Lila, like you are having some really big feelings; feelings of anger," to which Lila would respond with a kick to the shins and a dramatic stomp-off. Ramona and Frank would look at each other, baffled and upset. They were working so hard to use all of the right and positive phrases; why was their child so mean?

Finally, we have the classic city parent (or in suburbs or anywhere, really), where the child starts joining activities at age two and never stops. This accounts for almost every parent I know (including myself), and they usually follow an odd hybrid of Tiger and Mindful and Positive Parenting styles. Activities and sports only get added to the family's lives; nothing comes off the plate. The parents are working and driving and driving and working, and the child is beginning to whine about everything. If you are really lucky, the child will outright tell you they are tired. This is a gift from the child, but parents are petrified of what "quitting" means, and so the beat goes on until either parent or child has something close to a nervous breakdown. No one sees it coming, and yet . . . in hindsight it is clear as day. The mindless need for "more" is hurting many families; they just look so shiny from the outside.

The mindless need for "more" is hurting many families.

Now, back to the original question: What do I actually believe in when it comes to a parenting theory?

All. None. I believe that paying attention to the true needs of you and your children is the theory that is needed.

But lest you think that I don't have a specific point of view of parenting, don't worry, I do. In my early work life, I began as an outcomes-based counselor (it made sense for a school setting), and I then folded in Adlerian theory as my work with parent education grew. I became increasingly dissatisfied with these theories because *all* of the theories I studied had a nugget of truth, but the strategies I assigned *kind of* worked, but not with enough predictability. So, why did the application of these strategies and theories so often fail? What was missing? I wanted to go deeper; I wasn't interested in helping parents *just* control their children's behavior, I wanted to know *why* children behaved the way they did. What were the deeper impulses and needs that drive *all* humans to behave as we do? And how can this knowledge help parents?

Understanding Parenting Through the Developmental/Attachment Lens

In 2013, I attended a conference with Dr. Gordon Neufeld as the keynote speaker. I didn't go to hear him; there were numerous speakers I wanted to meet and I thought, *Meh, I will sit through him; see what he says.* Well, he changed my life. Only twice in my life have I listened to someone speak and reacted with a kind of epiphanic awakening (the other being my Buddhist teacher, Karen Maezen Miller), so as soon as he finished speaking, I signed up to study with him. After an extensive application, I was accepted into the two-year program to become a Neufeld facilitator. Without a doubt, studying in the Neufeld Approach did two things that changed my life as a parent and a professional. First, I made friends with uncertainty and how important it is to embrace *not knowing* as parenting growth instead of failure, and second, the Neufeld Approach uncovered the missing piece in the puzzle of my parenting work: the indisputable and deep need for connection between all humans. Most parents would *say* that they know connection is important, but many aren't living that out in their day-to-day interactions with their children. To study connection in a deeper way, well, it changed my life forever.

What is this magical theory that so greatly changed my life? The Neufeld Approach accounts for both development of the child as well as the basic theories of attachment (again, this is not Attachment Parenting), and how these two dynamics come together to produce a mature human. What does this mean for parents? The way we *attach* (essentially show loving warmth to our children) facilitates development and this has implications for everything when it comes to childhood and beyond. Secure, loving, and boundaried attachments directly contribute to children's ability to grow into patient adults who understand others' perspectives, share appropriately, have empathy, care about their surroundings, want to work hard without immediate reward, and have the ability to see the ambiguity in seemingly black-and-white situations. Secure attachment is pretty important, right?

Looking at childhood through this developmental/attachment lens greatly impacts how one understands children's behavior. Rather than only being concerned with the behavior and how to control it, this theory requires that you go deeper, past what you see, and look into what is *causing* the behavior. An analogy: Let's say your child is perpetually thirsty. Even when they haven't been exercising and there is no heat, when there are no obvious reasons for the thirst. If you don't understand why they are thirsty, you will keep giving the child water and they will continue to thirst. But let's say you step back and really look at the whole picture, and you see that your child is always asking for water and juice, and they are drinking the whole cup as soon as you give it to them. You begin to research and see that this could be a symptom of other needs, for instance, childhood diabetes! If this is the case, will more and more water help your child's condition? No. Your child needs an insulin balance; the water will never satisfy the deeper need!

By understanding your child's deeper needs, you can provide the needed connections and strategies that satisfy what is truly lacking. Sometimes those deeper needs aren't really all that deep or profound. For instance, your standard two-year-old? The one who won't stop throwing herself on the floor in a total meltdown? Yeah, that is common for the age. Do these tantrums require deep analysis and complex strategies? No, not usually. The only thing you can really do for a tantrum is (1) try to prevent and sidestep them *if you can*, and (2) don't make the tantrum worse when it is in progress by punishing, talking too much, or using logic. Are there some cases when there could be a medical or psychological or environmental cause for the tantrum? Yes! So, it is always worth the effort to zoom out of a problem and ask, "What is really happening here?" But honestly, tantrums are an expected and inconvenient part of raising preschoolers.

In order for you to read this book and get the most out of it, I must make this point crystal clear: **Every technique I use in my parent coaching and personal life, whether it be from behaviorism (rewards or punishments) or positive psychology (emotion coaching), seeks to deepen the connection between the parent and the child.** If the strategy seeks to emotionally divide parent and child, I will not use it. Do you sometimes need to be physically separated from your child so that you won't cause harm? Yes. Not only is that okay, but separation can actually be a form of connection. By taking a break to cool down, you are preventing yourself from saying and doing things that will hurt your relationship with your child. Yes, you are physically disconnecting for a moment (and remember, we are trying to parent for the long game here), but what you don't say and do is often as or more powerful than what you do say and do. (More on this later . . .)

I think the reason I was (and still am) attracted to the Neufeld Approach is that it does not give too many explicit strategies. The one-size-fits-all approach to parenting is what gets us into a lot of parenting pickles, as well as leads us away from our intuition. One-size-fits-all has us focusing on the wrong thing: the strategy instead of the child. Instead of understanding the interior world of the child, we keep trying to jam a strategy on them (the time-out being the most obvious example of a strategy that doesn't work for most children). When the child doesn't acquiesce to our strategy, our frustration grows, but the frustration is misplaced. We think the child is not adhering to this great strategy when, in fact, it's like forcing a square peg into a round hole: It just won't ever work.

The Neufeld Approach isn't strategy heavy, and neither is this book. In fact, you will read chapters where it seems like I am offering contradictory advice or outlooks. That's okay! I am not trying to be difficult or cagey; it is simply the case that one child's medicine is another child's poison. The last thing I want is for you to read in this book, "DO THIS!" and have it not only epically fail, but also hurt your relationship with your child. It is paradoxical, but the more comfortable you become with keeping your relationship with your child as your North Star, the more comfortable you will feel in the gray zone. Not knowing what to do will actually begin to feel like an invitation instead of the blind panic it may be now. Keeping connection as your goal frees you from having to act *right now* and respond to *every single problem.* You will find space and grace. You will more easily forgive your missteps, own and learn from your mistakes, and move forward confidently.

Don't worry, I *do* think a quick fix is often appropriate in our parenting lives and I will sometimes offer one.* Just don't look for too many prescriptive tips in this book. You don't need them.

What Are You Going to Get Out of This Book?

This book runs the gamut of parenting issues, from the mundane to the significant. I am truly writing from my heart to yours. I am writing to every parent who has cried and laughed and shared their stories with me. Every issue in this book is a problem or quandary that countless parents have brought to me, as well as issues that I have faced throughout parenting my own three children.

I am writing an answer to the thousands of letters I have received as a parenting columnist for the *Washington Post*. Every single parent who has ever written to me reaches out in the universal hope of something better: an easier way, a different path, more connection, and less upset in their family.

I wanted to write a book that feels like a back-to-basics book, but one where the "basics" feel more fresh and relevant.

I wanted to write a book that you would *want* to read while you snuggled into your bed.

I wanted to write a book that didn't make you feel like crap or like a failure (at least, not on purpose . . . your thoughts and feelings are your own).

I wanted to write a book that may challenge you, but not panic you.

I wanted to write a book that would make you laugh. Or at least

---

* Dr. Dan Siegel and Dr. Tina Bryson have written awesome strategy books (such as *The Whole-Brain Child*, among others) that are clear, kind, and empirically based when it comes to helping parents understand and work with children. I also like the basic strategies in the Positive Parenting books, such as Dr. Laura Markham's work and Jane Nelsen's work. In the back of this book, I will offer resources to help you find the right people to help you.

smile. So much of our parenting life is such a bizarre mess, filled with gross body fluids and other physical and emotional indignities. We need to remind ourselves that we (mostly) *chose* this life! We need to have a good laugh about it.

I wanted to write a book that shares my own parenting failures and wins. True, I have to protect my family and their privacy, but whenever I can, I want to share how I have folded my professional life into my own perfectly flawed parenting life.

I wanted to write a book that you may disagree with, and those disagreements would still provide a path for you to discover your own parenting voice. Not mine. Not Brené's. Not Oprah's (even though she has no kids, she is still a gold standard of how to *be*, generally speaking). Just little old you. Just good enough you.

This book does not contain:

- Hyper-specific parenting strategies

- Any specific current parenting trend

- Over earnestness or hand-wringing

- Attempts to make every parent happy (the death knell of any parenting book)

Oh, and a little tip while you read this book: Mark it up.

What happens when I read a great book (parenting or otherwise)? I always read it in bed. I will read a sentence that will make me sit straight up, grab a pencil/highlighter/pen, and underline the sentence. Sometimes I will scribble in the margins. I often fold down the corner of the page. And I always sit back and just let the words swim around. Since the feeling is almost always akin to being hit by a brick, I have to wait a minute and let everything settle (like muddy water, waiting for the dirt to drift to the bottom), and inevitably I say something like, "Holy moly, this is what I feel all the time." I will often cry with a spontaneous feeling of being overwhelmed, a feeling of vulnerability . . . like feeling exposed with a spotlight. But this is good, because it means something is shifting; something has happened and what I have experienced cannot be undone. I mean, sure . . . I can deny, deflect, and defer what has happened, *but I know that something has shifted in me.* Period.

So, I have left some room for you in the margins; go ahead and scribble. I've also included journal questions for you to ponder and answer for yourself, preferably in longhand. And I will repeat this throughout the book . . . moving information, thoughts, or feelings from your mind to your hand, into a pen, and onto a page *changes* something. Handwriting activates the same part of your brain that meditates, it strengthens working memory, and helps slow your worry (that's great for all of us parents who tend toward anxiety). Even reminding yourself of something on a sticky note is powerful, so if you feel sparked, write it down. *Something* is happening, and it is beneficial to let it sink in and swim around that brain of yours. Okay, let's get started!

CHAPTER 1

You Are Not Up to the Parenting Task, and You Never Were (and Other Lies Our Parenting Culture Will Tell You)

In much of America today, the parenting culture picks up speed early and never seems to slow down. As soon as you become pregnant . . . no, as soon as you *couple up*, it seems that the entire world rises up and sends you website after website of activities you and your child will need to do, ASAP. Oh, it begins innocuously enough when you are pregnant: You take one birthing class, but then comes Home Birth and Water Birth classes, then Breastfeeding, Baby Wearing, and Going Back to Work After Childbirth classes, and the next thing you know you're signed up for Knitting with Baby, Goat Yoga and Baby, Breastfeeding and Tequila Tasting, and Sleep Training Your Puppy and Baby classes. Taken alone, there is nothing wrong with any of these classes; it's just that all of these options begin to set the tone for what a "good" parent looks like in our modern culture, and that look is super jacked up.

For a long time (when I was blissfully childless), I really judged these activity-crazed parents. You know, the parents who relentlessly pursued every class and course; for whom self-improvement was a way of life. "What happened to you to make you *this* insecure?" I would muse as I watched these parents rush around the city. "These poor, poor parents . . ." My pity was more obnoxious than their insecurity, really, but I couldn't see it. (That's how obnoxious people are, right?) I simply could not understand why parents needed to spend their money and time on Mommy and Me Exercise and Baby and Bach and Swimming with Your Six-Month-Old and Baby Massage 101. Like, you don't know how to touch your baby? My snark was backed up by my childless friends and, like every non-parent who came before us, we would nod and smile to ourselves over our wine and crudités, accumulating our bad parenting karma. "We won't be like that as parents. Ever."

Ah, well.

Despite my laissez-faire attitude toward all things parenting when I wasn't actually a parent, as soon as my spouse and I decided to become pregnant, I found myself spiraling down dozens of "How to Conceive" websites. There were Chinese gender calendars, sex positions to guarantee a boy, analysis of monthly mucus (insert gross face here), and charts to track your temperature. My breezy "just have sex and see what happens" attitude was hijacked, and suddenly, I was part of the crowd. What crowd, you ask? The very crowd that I had made fun of, that's who. The crowd of people who tell you that you need tools and tricks and worksheets to get pregnant. I ate it up, and because every snarky person is actually a fearful person, my deep fear was that I could not get pregnant. There was zero evidence to support my thinking, mind you. By all accounts, I had a normal period and a normal ovulation and I had somehow escaped all versions of STIs and STDs in my teens and early twenties. I didn't have cysts or PCOS or endometriosis. My mother had easily conceived, as had her mother. I was in my mid-twenties and, true, I smoked cigarettes like it was my job and, yes, I drank enough alcohol to kill a horse . . . but otherwise, I was in good shape . . . right? None of those facts mattered. I was afraid I couldn't get pregnant because our culture *told me I needed to make it a project*, so into the interwebs I dove.

I love a project, so I began fastidiously tracking my temperature. Every morning, before my feet hit the floor, I would take my temperature and write it down on the sheet I had printed out. I was meticulous on the time and, as I went along, I noticed my temperature had begun to rise, if only slightly. Ah, good! I was ovulating! And as I went along, my temperature stayed slightly elevated. *Hmmm*, I thought, *I got this wrong. Something is wrong with this thermometer; my temp is supposed to drop again . . .* I was just trying to get a baseline going, and I had screwed that up. I showed my husband the chart, and he shrugged and suggested starting again after my period. I was discouraged. I had been off my pill for a month or two, and I guessed that the hormones were still messing with my system. I felt like I was already failing pregnancy school; it was just one simple and lousy worksheet with temperatures and dots on it, and I had already gotten it all wrong.

So, I went back to life as normal: smoking and drinking and waiting for my period. Despite my screwup, I was determined to get this temp thing right, but in the meantime, I felt like crap. My breasts hurt. I felt crampy and tired, and not just hangover tired. Like, dead-on-my-feet tired. Every opportunity I had, I was in the supine position. And when I could not lie down, I would put my head in my hands and just shut my eyes. I was teaching English literature in an all-boys school at the time, and I can remember the feeling of resting my head on the cool wooden desk as I waited for the boys to filter in. I remember wondering, *How many movies can I show them before the school fires me?* And food began to taste, well, odd. It was either like heaven on earth, or total dirt. I couldn't even swallow some of my favorite foods. *Must be getting the flu,* I thought.

Driving home on a Friday, I complained to my friend Caitie (a new mother herself) and in her typical and direct fashion, Caitie suggested the obvious: "It sounds like you're pregnant, Meg." No, I assured her, that couldn't be. I had screwed up the temperature thing, and I was just waiting for my period. *Wait, where was my period?* I silently wondered. Caitie sounded confident, so I stopped at CVS and bought the cheapest pregnancy test I could find. *There,* I thought. *I will take the damn thing, prove her wrong, and that will be that.*

The next morning, I peed on the stick, lit a cigarette, and proceeded to watch a *Real World: Paris* marathon on MTV. For hours, I laid on a futon (oh, the humanity), smoked cigarettes, drank peach-flavored Snapple iced tea, and watched a TV show that I had already watched that year. When the four iced teas finally caught up to me, I returned to the bathroom and saw the pregnancy test perched innocently on the edge of the tub. It was now late into the afternoon; how had I forgotten that I had taken a pregnancy test? Two lines. Wait, what did that mean? I began to feel the bottom dropping out of my stomach and rummaged through the trash for the pregnancy test box and instructions.

"Two lines equals pregnant," said the box. Well, the second line was kind of faint. "A faint line indicates pregnancy. See your doctor."

I dropped the test on the floor and turned to leave the bathroom, promptly tripping over my jeans. As I hit the floor, my breasts aching and my stomach churning, I remember thinking, *But I didn't do the temperature thing right . . .* Yes, of course I was pregnant. And looking back, this was just the first in a long line of incidents where I would not listen to my body or my instincts when it came to parenthood.

———————————

What does my pregnancy story have to do with your children and your activities? My point is that when it comes to trusting our intuition and what we know about our own children, our culture keeps us, the parents, in a whipped frenzy of doubt. We feel like we have to follow a certain path, instructions, and add more to our lives to live up to society's expectations. The message is clear: *You are not good enough to conceive, birth, and raise your own child.* Our logical brain knows this isn't true, but our emotional brain (our limbic system) whispers, "But what if you are wrong . . . ? The stakes are too high . . . This is *my kid* we are talking about! I have one shot to get this right . . . I don't wanna mess it up." Parents of all stripes and types are funneled into a tight cattle chute of choices and activities until our instincts are completely squeezed out of us.

The funny thing about the conception chart and the parenting activities I ended up throwing myself into with gusto? I never had these parenting doubts growing up. Oh, sure, I had lots of other things going on in my head that were irrational and unhealthy, but I never questioned my ability to parent. It sounds like a form of brainwashing, but I grew up knowing I was built to be a parent. When the time would come, I would simply know what to do. I was raised by and with confident, strong women; women who didn't dither around and wring their hands about small parenting decisions. And if they did dither? The kids sure didn't know about it. As a child, I assumed that parents knew what they were doing, and even though my mother has since disabused me of that thinking, there was a confidence that was unquestionably imprinted on me. I was going to be a strong mother. It was my birthright, my lineage, and my expected role.

So, how did I fall victim to both legitimate and cockamamie information on the web? How did I so quickly lose my mothering mojo? And why did *you* lose your mind and join a million things, most of which were a waste of time and money?

There seems to be a gap between our biological function as a parent (the unconscious hormonal and emotional mechanisms; the unconscious knowing of how to feed and burp and love a baby) and the confidence required to stand up, stand tall, and find the feeling of "I've got this" within ourselves.

This space, this threshold, this slight wrinkle in our humanity, *this* is where we lose it. This gap between our intuition and our fear, this is where the temperature charts, the birthing classes, the books, the blogs, the experts, the articles, and the doubts seep and sneak in. Without even noticing it, our unconscious brain silences our *intuition* and turns toward insecurity instead . . . all without us deciding if that is best. There wasn't a moment when I really asked myself why I couldn't just try to get pregnant without a worksheet; I just skipped right over giving my own biology a try and went straight to the websites. Over and over, I have asked parents, "Did you know you needed (fill in the activity or extra parenting enterprise) before you started it?" And over and over, most parents have said, "Hmmm, I don't recall ever thinking about it." Of course, many parents have said, "Yes, I am prone to depression and needed a community right away" or "I grew up with all sorts of ob-gyn issues that pointed me toward needing extra resources." But most parents shake their heads and say, "I don't know . . . my mother's group thought that Urban Farming and Baby classes would be fun, and I ended up really far away from who I am and what I really needed." I get it. We all get it.

I am not saying every activity for a new parent is "bad." I am not blasting natural birth or baby massage or sleep training classes.

These classes are tools and as such they are neutral, and assuming that the instructor is knowledgeable and kind, the classes are fine. In fact, if you are out pounding the parental pavement, looking for connection and other like-minded parents, then kudos to you. The books and activities and experts aren't the issue. The true issue is this: Have you asked yourself if you *need* these tools? Are you aware of your own shortcomings and strengths? And . . . are you comfortable with the knowledge that you just won't know what you are doing for much of your parenting life?

After the humbling experience of having children and signing up for *all of the parenting classes,* and after coaching hundreds and hundreds of parents, one thing is perfectly clear: We are not as damaged and insecure as we think we are! We just aren't aware of how our brains work, and we have stopped trusting ourselves. Because we are highly susceptible to panic and fear, and because there is nothing in nature that makes us more panicky and fearful than having a child, we have created a cultural loop of fear and reaction, reaction and fear. Without meaning to, parenting has been turned into a business, and that business is monetizing our parental fear.

If you are a typical parent and you ask yourself what you think is really true when it comes to parenting, you will likely swing from one extreme to another:

I am in too many "self-improvement" parenting activities.

I have too many books about parenting.

I am always an insecure mess and cannot change.

I worry too much.

Everything extra is getting thrown out. I am on my own from now on. I can do this.

I don't need anyone or anything.

Hold on . . . no, no, no!

I am 100 percent not interested in you giving up everything you are doing to enrich your parenting life. As much as it isn't healthy to go wherever the parenting trends are blowing you, it isn't healthy to eschew every activity or group or class that comes your way, either. Remember what I said in the introduction? We humans need community, we cannot live without it.

When I signed up for my first parenting class, I desperately wanted to be told what to do and when to do it. *Just give me the answers* was the message that ran through my mind as I wrote the check. *Just tell me how to get my daughter dressed for school. Just tell me how to stop screaming all the time.*

But the true skills and wisdom that I learned came from listening to my gut, the other parents, as well as the nuggets of wisdom from my teachers. Over time I learned how to take what I needed and leave the rest. My hope is that you read this book, take what you need or want, and disregard the rest. Just believe you are up to this parenting challenge. You can do this.

What are some small ways you can opt out of the parenting panic that's consuming our country? Here are some ideas! Read all the following thoughts, then write out the answers that come to you or just jot in the margin. You don't have to answer every question; this isn't a test. Just be authentic and honest.

REFLECT AND WRITE

1. As classes and activities and talks and lectures and groups arise and come across your desktop, are you confident enough to say, "No, thank you" first? You can think about an activity or expert or class and then, days or weeks later, join.

2. Ask yourself, "Do I want the activity or do I want to be around the people?" It matters not what you choose (or if you choose both), just try to clarify and know the difference. It is important to recognize your true need.

3. Do you truly have the money and time for the activities that interest you? Most parents I know (myself included) find a way to monetarily "make it work" when it comes to just about everything, but we aren't talking about PT for your child's low core strength here (which is an activity that probably falls into the "needed" category). Stretching yourself too thin is not in anyone's best interest.

4. Are you befriending people who ground you? Or do they keep you twisting in the wind of parenting anxiety? There was a time in my life when I was surrounded by friends who matched or fed my own anxieties. It didn't end well

for me, and I realized I had to let go of some of those friendships. In doing so, I was able to stop spinning my own wheels of worry. Sadly, among the list of people who keep you twisted up are sometimes family members. Don't throw them all away; just recognize how much energy you are giving these people and *stop doing that* (if you feel chronically anxious and belittled). Stop asking for and receiving their advice. It's that easy and that hard.

5. And here's a simple but worthwhile question: Do your activities bring you joy? Joy and happiness are usually the last categories we think of checking off, but what if we bumped them up to the top of our parenting list? If Underwater Basket Weaving and Baby brings you joy, then do it. If you love sitting on the sidelines of pee-wee soccer (and your child loves it, too), then do it. If you love being a classroom parent, then do it! And give yourself room for change, as in "I used to love being on the PTA and now I would rather poke my eyes out than sit in another meeting." Your life has seasons; embrace them.

6. Do you find yourself spiraling into anxiety? Can you talk to a therapist? It is healthy to talk to someone who is compassionate yet impartial about your troubles. It moves the chaos inside to the outside, where you can unpack it a little. Can people overdo it on therapy? Sure, but I generally find that more, not fewer, people need therapy.

CHAPTER 2

Sometimes You Need to Abandon a Full Grocery Cart in the Middle of the Aisle

I once left a cart full of groceries (you name it: frozen, fresh, and canned) smack in the middle of the aisle. Right there, in the congested grocery store.

My eldest child, Sophia (who was two at the time), was not having this grocery store visit from the moment I unclicked her car seat. We had already been running errands, as well as attended a Music Together class, but I just needed "a few things for dinner." Even just typing that right now is as much of a lie as it was twelve years ago. I *knew* I needed about $300 in groceries, but in my need to get it all done, I told myself, *This will be quick, just in and out.* It was a classic overparenting move if ever there was one, and from the arched back to the thrashing legs to the blood-curdling screams, there was no question about how my daughter felt about this impromptu errand.

It wasn't as if she went into the store sunny and happy and changed course once in the store; no, from the get-go, this trip was going to be a disaster.

But because I was an inexperienced and determined parent (see also: stubborn as hell and controlling), I was going to get the food.

By the fifteenth minute into the store, I was in a full flop sweat. The lollipops had been offered to and rejected by Sophia, and the shoppers were openly glaring at me and my devil-child. Whatever shopping list I had disappeared into the bowels of the grocery cart, squished and torn between apples and hummus. I was frantically trying to keep my daughter in the cart, scan the shelves, all while trying not to meet the eye of one other human. My panic, as well as my irrational anger toward every shopper in the store, was growing, but I would not let this little girl get the best of me. I would not allow her to dictate the success of my grocery trip. I needed food, and food I would procure, come hell or high water.

You know where this story is going, right?

As I leaned over to pick up the Cheerios (always on the bottom shelf), my daughter got to her feet in the cart. I turned to catch her as an older woman made a sound somewhere between a gasp and a shriek. More alarmed by the woman than my daughter, I cried out one of the worst curses that an Irish Catholic girl can say: "Jesus Fucking Christ!" The woman's hand flew to her mouth, my daughter kicked me in the gut, and just like that, I came to. Like coming out of a fever dream, I blinked, looked at the cart bursting with food and the horrified woman, and immediately knew: *I have to get the hell out of this store.*

Tossing my daughter over my shoulder like a sack of potatoes, I snatched my diaper bag, walked to the nearest grocery clerk, and said, "I am sorry. I have to leave. I am not coming back for those groceries." He took one look at my daughter, nodded, and I ran out of the store, eyes cast down, and my face aflame with embarrassment and failure. I was enraged at the older woman who scared me, I was enraged at my daughter for being such a two-year-old, and most of all, I was enraged at myself for pushing this agenda upon my child, everyone in that store, and myself.

But . . .

I did leave the cart.

Leaving that grocery cart was one of the best parenting decisions I had ever made because, of course, the cart was just the cart, but leaving it in the middle of the aisle has come to mean so much more to me than that one simple act. It was my first lesson in how detrimental my overparenting mentality could be, and it was my first lesson in learning to stop pushing, pushing, pushing my agenda. How? For instance, I believed that if I started a job, I needed to finish it. My child was along for the ride and she needed to learn that her needs were secondary to whatever task was at hand. If you had asked me point-blank: "Meghan, do you care that your daughter is miserable while you shop for yogurt?" I would have told you, "Yes, of course I care," but what I didn't realize was that deep down, my unconscious fears screamed, "If you give this child an inch, she'll take a mile." My act of shoving my daughter into the cart, my anger toward my fellow shoppers, my irrational stubbornness, and yes, my profuse sweating (my body's way of telling me, "Whoa, you are really in a panic here . . .") was driven by unspoken rules that simply were not true.

The food wasn't worth the disconnection with my child.

In fact, after I ran to the parking lot and clicked my daughter into her car seat, I stood outside my car and ordered a pizza. As my daughter unraveled in the car and my heart rate began to return to normal, I knew that a pizza would temporarily solve my problems. *And that was good enough.*

From that point on, "leaving the cart" became a North Star in my parenting life. It is a metaphor for these very questions: "Am I pushing because there is a true need or am I panicked over an irrational fear or expectation? And is my pushing adding to or subtracting from my relationship with my child?"

> "Am I pushing because there is a true need or am I panicked over an irrational fear or expectation? And is my pushing adding to or subtracting from my relationship with my child?"

The interesting thing about my "leaving the cart" anecdote is that, when I share it with other parents (and clients), the parents naturally tell me about their perspectives on controlling their kids (or lack thereof). For instance, some parents will remark, "Oh, I could never do that. I mean, I need those groceries. My child would have just needed to deal! Kids needs to learn how to suck it up or they will own you." Aha! Yes, I know this parent! Hi, my name is Meghan; nice to meet you, my fellow control freak.

And some parents, upon hearing my "leaving the cart" story, heartily agree with leaving the cart. "Oh yes. Always leave the cart. Who needs that drama? I don't go anywhere if I even think it might be too stressful. Life is too short to suffer." I know this parent, too. I married him. This parent is mortified by stress and outbursts, and often caves in the face of the smallest pushback.

And yes, there are the very rare parents who are actually in the middle (and parent from the middle a good bit of the time): "Yes, there are times when you need to just leave the store, but there are times when you must push through, doing the best you can." And, as you can guess, these parents tend to not be my clients as they manage to find equilibrium and serenity in the ever-changing parenting landscape of awareness and decision-making.

Here's the thing: When I left the cart in the store, I didn't make a *good* or a *bad* decision. I made a decision based on my real life, right in front of me. Not the stories in my head, not what a parenting expert thinks I should do, not what my guilt, shame, and ego were saying. And the reality was that there was no food needed badly enough to continue shopping in that kind of misery. I was damaging my relationship with my child and, as importantly, creating an untenable standard for myself.

When I speak to parents about staying attentive to *what is real*, when I ask parents if they can "leave the cart" in their own parenting lives, the number-one worry I hear is: "But won't I become inconsistent?"

Our parenting culture loves to go on and on about consistency, but mostly, we've got it all wrong. Consistency only works if you understand what is happening in front of you with clarity and compassion. Reacting to your fears, old stories, or someone else's notions of how you should be parenting means that you are consistent: Consistently *wrong* in your assessment! And therefore you're applying rules and consequences that don't support you or your child.

Instead of clinging to a strict set of rules, "always dos," and "never allows," we would be well-served to ask ourselves, "Can I leave this cart behind *in this instance?*"

Can I stop fighting with my child about brushing his teeth because this is not a real *crisis right now?*

Can I leave my child alone when she is struggling with her homework to see if she can work it out?

Can I stay quiet while my child plays soccer (even when she is playing very well and my cheering is considered "fine")?

Can I intervene when my child is chronically unkind to her best friend?

Can I apply the consequence when my child did not do his chore?

Can I audibly and aggressively push my agenda and my lesson to be sure my child heard it?

Some of these answers are yes, and some of these answers are no. For instance, say you have five-year-old twin boys who seem to spend 90 percent of their time wrestling. It often ends in tears, but they also usually get back up and go play. Do these children need to be disciplined or do you *feel* like they should be disciplined? Do you trust that they are sorting it out? Can you assess the needs of the situation, watch, and wait?

Or say the school has called and your ten-year-old daughter has been teasing and excluding a fellow classmate. Do you leave this alone and hope she sorts it out, or do you call a meeting with her and get curious about her relationship with her classmate?

Or say your eight-year-old whines about going to baseball practice every single week, to the point where he clings to your leg and begs not to go. Even after you drag and bribe and threaten him to practice, he mopes around, doesn't listen to the coach, and puts in no effort. Can you accept the juice ain't worth the squeeze and just quit the season? Or do you *feel* like you have to finish the season?

Figuring out what is actually going on with your child and your parenting is nuanced! Unless death and/or severe damage to body or home is imminent, you have wiggle room in every single parenting decision in your life. When you realize that you have choices and are not bound to a set of false parenting standards (like consistency), you are then freed from insecurity and doubt. You are freed from over-parenting and you can listen to your own intuition.

You can parent without limits, and what remains when you stop limiting yourself? The freedom to be the boss of yourself.

That day in the store, I could not force my child to sit down (without Child Protective Services being called on me). I could not force my fellow shoppers to stop staring (without the police being called on me). But I could choose to see myself clearly and pick another way to handle the situation. I could choose to change the only person I can actually change in this world: myself.

When you accept the reality in front of you, as well as the fact that you can only control yourself, you become more powerful than you can ever imagine. For instance, there was strength and power when I had to pin my daughter to a hospital table while they X-rayed her broken collarbone. Her shrieks were feral and my panic was at a point where rational thought had left me: I was all action, all doing, all quiet murmurs, all autopilot for the needs of the situation. If you have not yet done this kind of hard work, you will and you will know this focus and you will make it through. In that case, I could not "leave the cart." Her cracked collarbone meant I had to stay the course, not give into her screams and my panic. Our temporary suffering was serving a greater need, and I didn't need an expert to tell me that.

In fact, you hardly ever need a trend or an expert or a book to see and feel suffering. You don't need me to tell you when a fight with your child has gone too far or, conversely, to tell you when you have retreated from the hard work of parenting. I believe, in my heart, you know when you are out of alignment with your true parenting self: You feel shaky, unsure, doubtful, sweaty, headachy, rigid, sick, or sad. You have your own signs and warning signals that alert you to when you are out of sync with your parenting heart. The questions are: Are you seeing the signs? Are you listening to them? Are you feeling them?* It is more important for you to know yourself than it is for you to always know what it is you need to do. If you know your strengths, your weaknesses, your blind spots, your knee-jerk reactions, your Kabuki theater of parenting, you will probably see the needs of the situation with glaring clarity. Knowing when you are lost is actually different from simply being lost. It is the difference between being awake or asleep to your parenting life, and that difference is, well, everything.

It took a yelp from an old lady, as well as my own outburst, to awaken me to my daughter. Until that moment, I had believed that being "in control" equated "good parenting," and when this moment was revealed to me, it changed me forever.

Leaving the cart behind. Something to really think about, right?

REFLECT AND WRITE

1. Do you believe you have your own unique parenting intuition? Can you trust your intuition? How often do you push back or give up?

---

* I am aware that there are people who have experienced great trauma and/or have personality disorders that don't allow for much self-awareness and reflection. I believe every human is capable of growth, and I also allow that this growth looks different depending on your ability to access your feelings and emotions. If, while you are reading this book, you really don't know how you feel or cannot access empathy, please seek out the help of a professional therapist.

2. Do you panic and give in easily when the going gets tough with your children?

3. Do you armor up for every battle that comes your way, despite the obvious need to let some stuff go?

4. Do you feel like, "Nah, I got this; I am in the middle"?

5. What are your physical symptoms that you are out of step with your intuition? Do you sweat, clench your jaw, do your hands fist up, does your breathing become shallow, does your stomach hurt, do your shoulders rise to your ears? Do your best to slow down and understand the somatic reactions to feeling out of step (and yes, there are always reactions in the body).

CHAPTER 3

Just Let Them Wear the Pajamas! And Other Lessons I've Learned

Once upon a time, I was a mother with a two-year-old. That two-year-old was refusing to get dressed. After a particularly difficult wrestling match I like to call "trying to get my precious little one's shirt over her head so we could go to preschool," I realized I had hit my parenting rock bottom. I walked away from my child, locked myself in a bathroom, googled "parenting support," and up popped PEP (the Parent Encouragement Program). I called them as my two-year-old wailed on the other side of the door, and I calmly told the woman, Lynn, that my child refused to get dressed, she only wanted to stay in her pajamas, and I was at the end of my proverbial rope.

"Well," Lynn quietly asked, "why does she need to get dressed?"

"Because she needs to go to preschool," I answered.

"And . . . is there a possibility she could wear her pajamas to her preschool?"

My silence allowed my daughter's crying to reach the ears of the nice PEP lady, and hot shame raced up my neck to my cheeks.

"Are you there?" Lynn asked.

By this time, tears were rolling down my face. "Yes," I whispered.

"Sorry, I cannot hear you . . ." murmured the nice lady, though I was convinced she could.

"Yes! She could wear her pajamas, but none of the other kids wear pajamas and they all look cute and listen to their parents and nannies . . ." I whined. I knew I sounded like a brat, but why couldn't my child be like all these other kids? Why did everything have to be so hard?

"I know it is frustrating, and we can also stop watering the weeds," said Lynn. "You can just decide to let this pajama thing go."

Whoa. She was asking me to make a mature choice and that stung. I was not accustomed to "letting things go." In fact, my parenting and life style was more "dog with a bone" than "easy like Sunday morning," and I wasn't sure I knew how to let things go in my parenting world (or in any of my worlds).

What are the actual needs of the parenting situation?

This call changed my life. Within a week I found myself in a class with other suffering parents, and most important, I found myself with my soon-to-be friend Chrisy, a woman who would create a huge impact on my parenting life. A wise mom and a funny-as-hell woman, Chrisy taught the PEP curriculum with equal sass and seriousness, and I took it in like a sponge. Yes, I was still battling my child about issues that didn't really matter, but I was getting better at discerning when I had stepped over the line into insanity-ville. This discernment was due in large part to one key question that Chrisy would repeat multiple times in every class: "What are the actual needs of the parenting situation?"

As a perfectionist parent of a young child, *my* answer was clear and simple: The needs of the situation are whatever I said would happen and/or whatever I deemed as "needed." And guess what? My controlling nature mostly worked for me. For instance, those controlling ways made me an excellent parent to a baby. Decisive, confident, and strong, I instinctively knew what my baby needed. I knew what the different cries meant and I knew exactly how to react. I could anticipate sleep and hunger needs without thinking at all: I was a natural. I believed, in my heart, that I would know how to answer the parenting needs of the situation forever and ever, amen. My child was the question and I was the answer.

———————————

Fast-forward two and a half years, and I found myself in a parenting class because I expressly didn't know what the needs of the situation were anymore. Nothing, and I mean nothing, was going according to plan. Starting at two, my sweet child no longer seemed interested in taking directions from me. If I smiled and said, "Time to hurry up!" the child would immediately slow down. If I said, "Time to get those clothes on!" she would run away, shrieking with delight. Those perfect parenting instincts? Out the window. Forcing her out of pajamas and into "cute clothes" was my version of "good parenting" because, well, how could I let her be the boss of me? And once I decided I was the boss, she became the minion; once I decided that there would be a "winner" (me), that necessarily made her the loser. This kind of setup would never lead to anything but fighting and heartache, hence the call to the parenting program from the locked bathroom.

I could acknowledge that I was in over my head and my obvious need to control everyone and everything in my path was finally catching up with me (see Chapter 2 to understand this more), but here was the inherent problem I felt I was facing (and the problem of almost every amazing parent who calls me for parent coaching): If the needs of the situation were to stop fighting with a toddler about a shirt because (a) it was a glaringly stupid battle and (b) it obviously wasn't working to get my child dressed and (c) it was hurting our relationship, I was left with this important and crucial question: How was I supposed to get anything done in my house? More to the point, how was I to stay a leader of my family while still allowing flexibility, empathy, and change? How was I supposed to be the boss without being so darn bossy?

What was I supposed to *do*?

As I worked through the parenting class, one theme became wildly apparent: I was not going to figure out what to *do* in lieu of controlling myself and my child. I was not going to find an antidote or a new way or another answer while in this class. As I tried one strategy after another, as I watched some parents succeed as other parents failed, I began to see a clear theme emerge in myself as well as the other parents: *True humility was the way forward in this parenting journey.* It wasn't about being bossy versus being submissive, nor was it about happiness and joy. If I wanted to understand the needs of my parenting situations, I needed to become more humble.

The Power of Humbling Ourselves

How does humility (the "absence of pride or arrogance," per Merriam-Webster's) help me parent my child without being bossy or passive? For me, seeing how my own ego is in the way helps change the question from "What do I do?" to "How can I *be*?" For instance, how can I be when my daughter doesn't want the fancy shirt pulled over her head? I can be more empathic to her developmental needs, more understanding of how I am making her feel, and less vain in my pursuit for her to look "appropriate." Or, how can I be when my child demands she charges all of her technology in her bedroom, despite our house rules? I can be understanding of her feelings while also remaining steadfast in my rules about technology. I can see how she will fight my rules and I can choose to not take it (too) personally (cue door slamming and "This family *sucks*" outbursts). How can I be when my toddler throws a fit in a restaurant? If I take my ego out of it and humble myself, I will see that the tantrum isn't personally directed at me, and I can be loving while taking her out of the restaurant to spare the diners her feral screams.

Allowing humility to guide my parenting isn't about lowering myself or lowering my standards, nor is it about eschewing my own needs. True parenting humility allows for multiple perspectives of one situation, it allows for freedom of choice in the service of the greatest need, it allows for mistakes and forgiveness (of everyone), and it allows for the opportunity to learn and try again.

The parents who were "succeeding" in PEP, I noticed, weren't *doing* the techniques "just right." Instead, their eyes were wide open to themselves and their children. These parents were both creating situations that better suited their children, as well as responding to their children with less scripts and more authenticity. The parents who appeared more peaceful were making lots of mistakes, staying thoughtful and open, and maintaining a sense of humor. I was both amazed and envious of these parents, but I knew that I could become more like them; I knew I could begin to find more humility and trust myself more as a parent, but how?

It is hard (very, very, very hard) to make a leap into trusting your child and yourself, and most of us will have to "fake it till we make it." Faking it means that you have to sometimes pretend you are a humble and patient and trusting and benevolent and strong person before you regularly become that person. You have to say rehearsed words (even though that seems to fly in the face of what you think you should be doing), and you have to use strategies that trick you into believing this new way of thinking. Oh, you don't think this works? It does! All of the time! As an example of this, take my foray into the yoga world: I started yoga in sweatpants and a poorly fitting sports bra under a big T-shirt. I felt like a wannabe yoga loser, and I didn't feel like I belonged with all the other women, what with their beautiful asanas and fancy leggings. I knew I had a long way to go in my yoga practice, but in the meantime, I bought some cute yoga pants and a proper yoga top. I still sucked at yoga and felt insecure as all get-out, but when I saw myself in the mirror, my mind exclaimed, "Now, there's a yogi." I smiled and felt good about myself, and guess what? That makes for a better yoga practice! Fellow yogis would notice my confident smile and leggings and remark, "Cute pants." I belonged! I was becoming a yogi (or on my way); I was faking it, with pants and whatnot, until I really felt like one. Would I have eventually gotten into an unassisted Half Moon pose in sweats? Yes. Was it easier to achieve that pose because I had decided I was a yogi and could do it? Yes!

Parenting is not so different from my yoga experience. We are asked daily to find language for a scenario we have never encountered before with children we are still getting to know. Not only is it appropriate to humble ourselves and feel okay with not having all the answers, but we can also assume that we can fake it until we make it. We can fake having humility and confidence before it comes naturally. Practicing how to "be" rather than assuming that we always know what "to do" works! How else can we fake humility until it feels more natural? How can we trick our brains into believing that we can change, even if it is little by little? Let's take it back to the start of the chapter.

I came to the parenting classes with the realization that I was an egomaniac control freak who was forcing clothes on my daughter and calling it "parenting." Chrisy taught me to look at the needs of the situation, but in order to more clearly see said needs, I needed to humble myself. How could I humble myself? How could I clear the cluttered sill of my ego? I was going to fake it.

Instead of simply trusting myself to remember how to be, I wrote myself reminders. A seemingly simple, kind of stupid yet highly effective strategy, I reminded myself, *every single day*, who I wanted to be for my daughter. Here are some samples:

> *Dear Meghan,*
> *Please be kind and allow Sophia to choose her own clothing. Even if, in that choosing, she never gets out of her pajamas.*
> *And when she refuses to put on normal clothing, smile and say, "Awesome. Time for waffles."*
> *Mean it when you say it. Hug her.*
> *Love,*
> *Meghan*

> *Lovely Meghan,*
> *Be aware that you are overly invested in your daughter's looks. Your daughter is not the sum of her cute outfits and pretty hair.*
> *Leave her alone and love her for who she is, today, right now.*
> *Love,*
> *Meghan*

Hi Meghan,

Please remember and be aware that Sophia likes pj's because they are comfortable and she is almost three, so comfort rules. There is nothing wrong with her. In fact, it is normal.

Stop trying to change her. Literally and figuratively.

Your friend,

Meghan

Yo,

Be grateful for this stage. Your daughter will eventually wear clothes that will make you die inside, so be grateful for this stage.

M

Were these notes a bit ridiculous? Maybe, but I didn't (yet) trust my own intuition or my ability to remember what I needed to do every morning; I needed a visual reminder to *be better.* I needed a note, an alarm on my phone, a journal entry, a mantra, a visual smack to the head, anything to snap my mind into what I really wanted to do and how I wanted to be. Otherwise? I knew I would be back to my old ways; I had been practicing being bossy for a good long while; one solid mental breakdown and a handful of parenting classes was not going to change me overnight.

But guess what? *It worked!* The notes actually worked! Despite my complete panic (I am talking sweat-running-down-my-back level of panic), days turned into weeks and before I knew it, my child and I stopped fighting about clothing in the morning. Yes, true, we could get into the occasional tussle about other inane issues, but I was no longer physically wrestling with her, trying to reward or threatening her, passive-aggressively offering false choices, or icing her out with my disappointment. I was just moving the morning along, focusing on what really mattered, and being the mom I knew my daughter wanted and needed.

And then, something truly amazing happened: I actually stopped caring about how she looked when we left the house. I stopped dragging a brush through her curls to go to the grocery store or the park (because, *honestly*). I didn't dress her up to go on a playdate or visit a neighbor. There was still syrup down her pajama top? So be it; it didn't matter.

I was truly agog. By humbling myself to see more of my child, to see the needs of the situation, and to trust my intuition, I experienced an actual values shift in my parenting life. I found a way to love her for exactly who she was. I enjoyed her more. We laughed more. I let some of the house go (and I never got it back, so maybe that isn't the best example, but whatever) and other parents started remarking, "You two seem to be having so much fun!" And we were! We really were. And it had nothing to do with a change I had produced in my child; this was a change within me.

Now, maybe you are worried that my child looked like a hooligan. Maybe you think my standards went too low. Maybe you think I let this humility thing go too far and that I created a monster. You believe I created a child who could not and would not dress in appropriate clothing for the appropriate occasions. So, let me tell you how this little experiment worked out: That two-year-old is now an older teen. She wears dresses and heels (maybe a tad too high for me sometimes) to events that warrant dresses and heels, such as bat mitzvahs, liturgies, funerals, graduations, and weddings. She wears nice pants, jeans, or shorts and a clean, nice-looking shirt to school or babysitting, and she wears leggings and cute tees to hang with her friends. Essentially, she looks like every other teen out there. I don't ask her to wear dressy clothes to church; she just does. I don't ask her to forgo the tiny crop top to babysit; she just doesn't wear it. Am I saying that I created a young woman who knows how to dress appropriately? No. I am saying that, *when I humbled myself and got out of her way, I stopped making a problem out of something that was not a problem.* I made room for her to grow into her own person. By allowing her the freedom to be truly comfortable as a child, by slowing my constant interference and judgment and critique and control, my child was still somehow able to figure out what she should wear to which event. It seems, despite my desire to control her, that my child could figure things out for herself. Huh. Imagine that. A human developing and maturing and growing without another human forcing them to do it . . . what a head-scratcher.

I want to encourage you, but I am going to be honest: Learning how to be before you figure out what to *do* is hard work, but you didn't have children because you thought it was going to be easy. You had children so that you could learn hard things about yourself, struggle, and then grow as a human (and if you didn't have children for that reason, well, now you know). And the reality for most of us? We (me) are going to struggle a lot more than others, and these struggles will take the shape of ridiculous topics (clothing on a two-year-old). You may have friends and family for whom parenting seems to be a natural extension of their already blessed nature. They appear to struggle less, be less angry, less reactive, less disappointed, and less yanked around by their emotions. Well, bully for them. Somehow, their genes and life experiences came together to create a stable person, a true unicorn (I married one; it is so annoying). The rest of us are anxiety-ridden, nerve-jangled, depressive, narcissistic, whining, and angry victims who simultaneously want pity and respect, revenge and accolades. We are fully human, and this will make humility and practice *hard*. But it also makes it more necessary and more worth it.

Addressing the needs of the situation and learning what to let go—these lessons are earned. These lessons are not delivered upon you like a strike to the head (although they sometimes feel like that), nor are they awarded to you because you have good intentions (though intentions are really important). Learning to see what the real needs of a situation are and consistently listening to your intuition is a one-day-at-a-time gig. It is a long-haul effort.

REFLECT AND WRITE

1. If you are a controller and see the need in *every* situation, where do you think that began? Stop and reflect for a while. Did it begin in your childhood? As an adult? When did you unconsciously want everything to be a certain way and begin to think of that as "caring"? Was there an event that led to this or was it a slow change? Or both? Don't try to assign blame to others, just ask and answer these questions.

2. Do the people in your life rely on you being in control and always knowing what the "needs of the situation" are? Who will be uncomfortable as you begin to change your controlling ways? Who will love it? Who may not even notice, and will that bother you?

3. What are the primary emotions you feel as a result of your controlling nature? Yup, list the good and the bad here. And a side note of interest: Often (but not all the time),

anxiety can manifest as a need to control; since we don't always know what we are anxious about, sometimes niggling around with both seemingly big and small issues in our family temporarily fulfills our ever-present need and worry. Anxiety also keeps us on high alert. Essentially, your brain is endlessly provoking and poking you, "Hey! That's a problem . . ." and "Oh, look! That's a problem over there!" and "Whoa! That's another problem, that kid of yours." You are the hammer, the kid is the nail, and meanwhile, your anxious brain is never, ever satisfied. To the outside world, you are looking A-OK! Controlling parents are often praised for their efforts, and it is hard to break free from this false praise. But remember: Controlling your child in every circumstance is not addressing the parenting needs of the situation; it is being a dictator. And it is exhausting and never-ending.

4.   When you think of the word "humility," what comes up for you? Does it have religious connotations? Negative connotations? Do you feel limited by it? Or freed? Why?

5.   What are you willing to do to really change this? Parenting classes in person or online, reading a book with a fellow friend or partner, therapy, coaching . . . you name it. What are you really willing and able to do? This depends on time (you have that, trust me) and money (that is a bigger consideration) and your willingness to acknowledge that your way isn't working (this is the biggest obstacle to change . . . our own brains). If you think, "Meh, I like the way I am," then so be it. But never forget that

small changes make a big difference! Even just allowing more space and compassion into a morning routine can bring more peace and joy to your family! We don't need big, sweeping changes to see improvements. Just be honest with yourself.

CHAPTER 4

Your Children Are Going to Fight and Yes, It Is Hard, and Yes, We Can Make It Better

The unexpected joy of having more than one child is experiencing sibling arguments. I know, because I have three girls. And they can fight. I'm not talking small tiffs, mind you, I am talking about the blowout fights between children who can only be related. I cannot believe that my girls share blood, so nasty have been the spiteful comments, kicks, and pushes of my own children over the years. And while my children are mostly loving and lovely people, the fighting has reached fever pitch. Often.

As they've gotten older, I have become accustomed to some of the arguments. I have learned when to defuse them and when to let them pan out. I have learned that one of the children may be like a hammer looking for a nail and needs some redirection stat, or that there are some serious beefs to be settled between two of the kids, and I need

33

to help them navigate the communication. One thing I know, for sure, is that I never fully understand *why* they are fighting. Trying to get to the bottom of hurt feelings is like spelunking with a match: You are not going to get too far.

As each of my children turned the corner of eight and nine years old, I began to notice something curious about the sibling squabbles. While the insults may have been thrown at the beginning of the fight, the kids would soon begin to show some reasoning skills. They would begin to find their feeling words and communicate in a way that showed they understood a different perspective. Without my interference (usually), my children began to regularly solve their own problems. And in case you think that this is particular to my own family, it isn't. I have worked with families for years where, with some consideration and thoughtful effort (from the parents), they have also watched their children go from daily brawls to only here-and-there skirmishes. How did this happen? How, with minimal effort from the parents, did the children find some equanimity in their relationships?

In order to understand how siblings (and all humans who live together) can communicate a bit more peacefully is to understand how emotions are processed in the body and in the mind, and how these processes are tied directly to development. We can also understand, as parents, how we can either interfere or assist with these developmental processes, hence promoting or hindering peaceful interactions among our children.

Let's take my beautiful daughter Gigi. Because she is the youngest, she needs to fight tooth and nail for her opportunities to talk and be heard. When she was younger, the struggle to be heard led to frustration on top of frustration, and her anger would explode easily. Her particular explosions often manifested in swift kicks to the shin because, while there were so many voices and so many people to speak over, a swift kick was going to put a quick stop to being ignored. Everyone stopped talking and all eyes went to Gigi.

Kicking also led to drag-out fights with her sisters. Because a kicked shin hurts like hell, soon smacks, hits, hair pulling, and pinching would ensue, and my children quickly became a rolling mass of screams and tears. As I pulled them apart, Gigi was the obvious person to blame. Her kick seemingly started the whole mess, but how was I to discipline her? She would weep as she described (as only a four-year-old could) how she *tried* to tell her sisters something important and how she *tried* to get their attention, but they just ignored her and pushed her away. She didn't want to kick them, but she simply felt she had run out of options. She *had* to kick them.

She was labeled as having the problem (and yes, the kicking was not great), but I also empathized with her. How was a four-year-old *supposed* to communicate with her older, taller, more mature and verbal sisters? How was she supposed to "know better" and, to that end, "do better"? On their best day, four-year-old's are intense creatures, full of chutzpah and shyness, creativity and boredom, independence and neediness. And so, while I wanted to create behavior charts and logical consequences, I knew that the frustrations were just too big for Gigi's four-year-old mind to handle.

You may be relating to this, because you have a child kicking or hitting or biting or spitting at their siblings. You are desperate to make it stop, but how? Your intuition may be telling you that your child is doing the best they can with the skills they have, but *violence is unacceptable*, right? That's at least what we have been taught. All of your time-outs and consequences and rational talks have failed spectacularly, even resulting in more frustration, and now you feel pretty hopeless.

How do we understand a young (or immature) child and violence when it comes to their siblings? Children under five (and sometimes six, seven, eight . . . or right into adulthood) struggle with their big emotions. When the frustrations of life and family overwhelm these children, any capacity for patience, empathy, and open-mindedness flies out the window and a physical manifestation of the frustration explodes, aimed squarely at the person who knowingly or unknowingly brought on the frustration. This limbic system overload is not a dysfunction nor is it even misbehavior; it is the human body reacting in the best way that it can.* But how do we help the immature child become less explosive with her siblings or friends? We cannot simply wait for time to do its work while the child beats everyone senseless. No, there have got to be other ways.

Zooming Out and Looking for the Patterns

Looking for the patterns of the drama is going to give you the most clarity most quickly in order to help yourself, your child, and the siblings. And when it comes to siblings fighting, looking for patterns is especially powerful because they are under your nose. Unlike school or sports issues, the sibling shenanigans are usually happening right in front of you, but because you are so conditioned to your own response, you aren't even looking for these patterns.

Seeing these patterns requires that you look through a wide-zoom lens. While it is only natural to see and respond to the *one* fight or only focus on *one* child, looking for all of the patterns means that you will begin to see that it is rarely only one child who is causing the problem. Looking for patterns can also do something truly magical: It can marry what you know about your children (your own

---

* The limbic system is a part of the brain that deals with emotions and memory. It regulates both autonomic or endocrine function in response to emotional stimuli and also is involved in reinforcing behavior.

intuition) with finding the right techniques to help the family (outside wisdom).

Here are some common patterns you may begin to notice as you zoom out:

Are your children sick, hungry, and/or tired? You won't believe how many clients I have had whose children were fighting *every day at 5:00 p.m.* because the children were starving and exhausted. The parent wanted to create consequence and punishment charts, take away the TV, as well as ban all desserts, but simply allowing the children to eat some carrots and crackers at 4:30 p.m. practically stopped all of the fighting in its tracks. Being hangry is real, y'all! Sometimes, the simplest response is the best response, and this goes for children of every age. We forget that, while there absolutely can be complicated challenges with our children's arguments, most of our parenting issues have clear reasons (hunger) and, therefore, require straightforward responses from us (food).

Are you actively favoring one child over the others? You may be surprised to learn how many parents favor one child in the family. And before you build out some abusive tale of woe and neglect, favoritism is often an unconscious act on the part of the parent. Maybe the parent and child share a temperament (both shy, as an example), maybe the parent and child both love music, maybe the child has an easygoing disposition, maybe the child has special needs that result in a special parental protectiveness and bond, or maybe the parent sees their loved ones in the face of their child. There are a million reasons why one parent prefers one child over the others, but the problem comes when the child is treated differently because of this favoritism. And when the children *feel* that one child is preferred, a whole host of misbehaviors and shenanigans begin, especially between the siblings.

One of the ways that favoritism adds to sibling fighting is open comparisons. We probably know that phrases such as "Why aren't you more like your brother?" are acutely painful, but they also feel like the script of a 1990s afterschool special, and I am not sure many parents actually *say* that these days. The comparisons I *do* hear are phrases like "Your brother is not afraid to swim. I know that you can also get in the pool. Let's go, get in." Or "All of your siblings are sitting and eating like normal kids . . . you can too, right?" Or "Your sisters *never* speak this way to me. What makes you think you can?" Statements like this are cancerous for your family. Not only is your child hurt by your words, but they now resent the sibling they are being compared to! And what's worse? The child who is being used for comparison often doesn't even know that they are being held up as the standard by which their sibling is failing! Being the "preferred" sibling is as damaging as being the "losing" sibling; pain from sibling comparisons ripple out through the entire family and can cause resentments and arguments that can cause generational resentment. It can be particularly painful to recognize this pattern, but take heart: By simply recognizing that you are favoring one child over another, you can spark an awareness that has the potential to undo many bad habits. While it may be hard to break the favoritism cycle, admitting you have a problem is a huge first step.

Are you creating unnecessary competitions? A spin-off of favoritism in families is the comparison game. It usually starts innocently enough: "Let's see who gets to the sink first to wash their hands!" "Let's race to the car!" "Whoever finishes their peas gets dessert first!" And it works! Your kiddos are running to sinks and cars, and shoving peas down their throats, and you are happy. The children are cooperating; they are doing what you want them to do. But you soon begin to notice a pattern emerging: One sibling is always winning and one sibling is always losing. And with this winning and losing comes whining, punching, crying, and then some stomping away. Huh. It seems the competition has morphed into an opportunity for hurt feelings, violence, and mayhem. And you find yourself disciplining the child who demonstrates the most anger—the sibling who has lashed out against the faster, smarter, or more patient sibling. (If this is your discipline method, go ahead and write those examples in the margin. It will help your brain.)

Is the child (or family) in the midst an important transition? While most people assume a transition is always "bad," it can also be an exciting new school, a new baby, a new marriage . . . all good changes! True, a transition can be an illness, a diagnosis, a death, or a divorce or separation, but parents often assume that the child will only "act up" when life is hard or sad. But change is change, and children require routine, structure, and balance to feel safe. When life throws that structure out of whack, many children feel this acutely and act up with their siblings. You may have a child in your family for whom the start of school comes with a bit of stress, but otherwise, they keep ticking along. You also may parent a child who holds it all together in school, only to come home and growl at every human in sight, picking a fight a minute with their siblings. And this can go on for weeks and weeks! Seeing the pattern of "change + child = explosions" at home can lead you to a whole set of strategies to bring your children some peace.

Is your child intense, gifted, anxious, or needs other emotional and/or physical supports? Whether diagnosed or on their way to diagnosis, the intense child can often have explosions of frustration, creating more frequent conflicts with their siblings. Intense children do not want to be difficult and argumentative, but day-to-day life tests them in ways that leave little room for emotional tests and patience at home. Imagine a cup, filled with all of a child's energy and good intentions: An intense child has been drip-drip-dripping his good intentions and energy all day with his teachers and fellow students, doing his best to pay attention and be "good." When he is confronted by even a whiff of crankiness from his sister, the child has nothing left in his tank for being kind and patient. All the child's good intentions are gone, and all that is left is frustration and anger, and that frustration and anger will be directed right at his little sister.

Similarly, you may have an acting-out child because they have a sibling with special needs. The family's resources, attention, and patience may largely go to the child who needs it the most, leaving the other children frustrated, confused, jealous, and hurt. These feelings may come out sideways, such as bullying another child in the house (often not the child with the needs) or whining about other children in the house.

Is your "problem" child being teased or pulled into another sibling's drama? This can be tricky to spot, but I have seen a child get labeled as the problematic sibling and, upon closer inspection, learned that the child was being pulled into an unseen drama and therefore had a reaction that just happened to grab all the parental attention. Here is an example: I have coached families where the whole family loves to be outside and doing, doing, doing. Then, there is one child who prefers a slightly slower pace in life. He may enjoy sitting quietly, reading, playing alone, or being around fewer people and less stimuli, and every time it comes to leaving the house, one of his siblings begins to needle him. "Come on, Robert. You are such a pain, just put on your shoes. Why do you always just want to sit around? Aren't you bored? You are making us late! Come on, Dad is going to come up here and yell at both of us!" Pretty soon, little Robert has had enough and has some sharp words and a shove for his sibling. Robert appears to be the "problem sibling" due to the shouting and shoving, but is he really the problem? Zooming out for the patterns shows us that Robert's sibling also has a strong hand in the back and forth of the struggles, and both children must be addressed to improve this situation. Period. Another example: There may be a child who is chronically disorganized and is always asking her sibling to help her find her things. As the other sibling tries to help, the unorganized child becomes increasingly overwhelmed and frustrated, eventually turning to the sibling, yelling, "Are you going to help me or not? You are useless!" And then we have a fight going!

Do your children know how to *positively* get your attention? When I hear that siblings are fighting *every single day* for the same parent, despite how smooth and structured things seem to be in the household, I quickly zero in on finding out if the children know how to communicate their needs to their parents without drama. Because children are immature and almost always want a parent's attention, they will do whatever works to get it. If every time brother and sister begin to fight over the remote and Mom comes in to scream at them, what has been reinforced? Loud fighting equals Mom's attention! The children aren't conscious that this behavioral groove has been paved in their brains; they just know that Mom is looking at them. So, day after day, fight after fight, the children have become accustomed to summoning Mom with their bickering. And lest you think that this happens with only young children, I have been working with a parent of two teens, and this happens every single day in their family (and we have figured out a way to help this parent connect to the teens with a little less drama!).

When it comes to this dynamic (chronic fighting for a parent's attention), I often see that one parent bears the brunt of the drama, whereas the other is spared. This dynamic causes a great deal of anxiety, resentment, and anger for the parent who feels nagged and victimized—they don't understand why they seem to be getting the raw end of the deal. *Why isn't the other parent struggling?* they wonder. I also see this dynamic (kids fighting to get a parent's attention) when one parent is significantly distracted for a long period of time (weeks or months). Maybe it is career stress, maybe it is depression, maybe it is sickness, maybe it is marital strife; whatever the cause, children are programmed to get a parent's attention and nothing gets it faster than whining, fighting, and crying.

Is there a structural or routine problem in the household? When I look for patterns with a parent, we reveal that a frequent cause of sibling struggles is that there are problems with the family routine. If there is a lack of routine and the children do not know what they are supposed to be doing, well, you know what happens when kids are bored: *fights*. Usually, the sib with the most energy/sassiness/ strength/smarts/leadership will rise to the top and start some mayhem with their brothers and sisters. This is not because the child is "bad" or wants to ruin the family, rather this is what happens when there is an absence of strong leadership and weak systems in the household. When the siblings feel insecure and lost, one child will often begin to boss the other children around (we call this child the "little mom" or "little dad" or "little parent" and will think it is cute . . . until it isn't), or make up games that quickly fall apart, or begin to tease the other siblings. Seeing this pattern is an easy way to find where and what strategies are best needed to eliminate confusion and therefore help the sibs stop fighting (as much).

In a similar vein, sometimes the parents realize that their household systems no longer work for their family. Maybe the routine worked last year when the children were younger, but now they need more independence, more responsibility, and more accountability. When siblings don't share assigned and discrete jobs or chores, this usually leads to a lopsided workload, and *that* usually leads to big fights. One older child may yell, "Why am I *always* folding all of the towels while Susan is off playing?" "Why is Kate always getting the easy chore?" "Why does Tony always whine his way out of his chore?" There are simple and easy ways to fix all of this, but first we have to see that this is the issue.

Conversely, a parent may see that they have a virtual stranglehold on the family routine and, therefore, the children's independence. The family routine doesn't allow for any wiggle room, and the children feel suffocated and frustrated. If the parents are too controlling, children may begin to pick fights with each other. The frustration has to go somewhere, right? I understand how our routines become stuck: You don't need to look too far to see that many families are overworked, overscheduled, and overcommitted, and there isn't a lot of time to assess your stagnant routines, let alone redo them. It can feel daunting to make changes, so it's easier to just keep moving forward with the devil you know.

Do you always seek an answer or try to place blame when the children are in a disagreement? Are you always creating punishments and consequences for your children when they fight? One of the quickest ways to lose your parenting mind is trying to get to the bottom of why your children are fighting. True, every once in a blue moon it is obvious that one child is at fault, but in truth? Many sibling disagreements you witness are just the tip of a much longer argument that has been rumbling below the surface for a long while. You simply don't know what led up to the kerfuffle. And the answers you are desperately seeking? Not there. To make it worse, the more you dig to place blame, the more your children will cry foul. No matter who ends up with the blame, they will be shocked and angry. They will scream things like, "You *always* side with Mary! She *never* does anything wrong, right? What a brat!"

Seeking logic in these emotional outbursts not only furthers the divide between your children but also leads to inadequate consequences. Because it is a guarantee that you have not read the tea leaves correctly, whoever gets punished will feel that a great injustice has been perpetrated against them. The child who has gotten off scot-free will wipe their tears, gloating the whole time, and meanwhile? Maybe some consequences were warranted, but we chose sides and now any point you are trying to make is lost on both children. The punished child is irate and planning revenge, and the free child feels chosen and arrogant. Trying to assign blame and create on-the-spot consequences will almost always lead to more sibling squabbles.

———————————

A little aside: I just gave you what may feel like one million reasons as to why your children are fighting. Your head may be spinning, but here is what I want you to know: Don't worry about it. Oh sure, chronically arguing children can be soul crushing and very distressing, and your mind may be whirling, but don't get caught up in finding one answer or one way. Just sleep or walk on it, just don't think too much. Remember, we are trying to find a way back to our intuition.

Disrupting the Patterns of Sibling Drama

You may have read Chapter 4 and thought, "I get it—I see why my children are fighting, and I know what to do about it!" Often, once we parents *see* the problem, the solution crystalizes right before our eyes. Or, sometimes we need more help, the zoom out is still muddy. This is neither good nor bad, right nor wrong, better nor worse, so don't judge yourself if you see the problem yet feel lost as to how to stop the sibling drama-llama. That's why I am here. Instead, let's peek at some of the insights you may have had:

Oh! I have created so much competition between my kids. I keep yelling at the kid who is always hitting, but he is sick of losing a game he'll never win!

My sensitive kid keeps getting teased by his more confident little brother. That sensitive kiddo is having trouble handling that.

Wow, I really gravitate toward my daughter . . . but she was just born so early. She was so little, I just cannot let her siblings hurt her . . .

My kids disagree here and there, but I flip out like a maniac whenever they get prickly with each other. I cannot handle any friction.

What can you do?

Stop It

So as to not panic you further, my first bit of advice for how to put a stop to the sibling fighting is going to be quite simple:

Stop it.

Have you ever seen the Bob Newhart skit "Stop It!"? If you are near a computer, check it out. Essentially, Mr. Newhart plays a therapist and a woman comes in seeking help for her problems. She is afraid of many things: being buried alive, driving a car, sabotaging her relationships, etc. Bob listens carefully, and when she is finished with her list, he says that he has a foolproof way to help her get over her fears and worries. Looking straight at her, he yells: "STOP IT!" The woman sputters, "But I am afraid I will be buried alive," to which he yells, "Well, STOP IT!"

While I do take psychological issues very seriously, this is a hysterical skit because there is a bit of truth in it for us. We live in an "add it in" and "fix all the problems" parenting culture, but there's a lot to be said for simply stopping what isn't working. Most of my coaching is encouraging, helping, and creating plans for parents to stop what isn't working (and never did).

If you pit your children against each other to accomplish a goal (like forcing a competition to get teeth brushed or get into the car) only to watch them melt down and fight every time? Stop it. Stop creating competitive scenarios. Stop asking them to race, and stop announcing, "Whoever gets their teeth brushed first gets the first story!" While we can add in some positive strategies to help these kids get along, doesn't it make more sense to stop creating the very competition that causes the fight? Take, for instance, the client whose children would not stop fighting and crying due to the chronic competition the parent had created around nearly every transition in the house. We pinpointed when the fighting was the worst and the parent *stopped* making the transition into a rivalry. He literally stopped using phrases like "Who can get to the dining room first?" or "Who can buckle in the fastest?" And while the parent was dismayed to see the mess he had unintentionally created, simply eliminating the competition was powerful enough to stop much of the fighting in its tracks.

Another behavior you, the parent, can stop? If you freak out every time your children get sick of each other, even when it falls into the typical range of sibling behavior? Stop it. Stop overreacting to human squabbles. Hang up a sticky note that says, "It is normal for humans to get sick of each other." Place a Band-Aid over your mouth (don't laugh, I have done it). Take out the trash or check a fake emergency in another room. Anything to stop you from saying the same thing over and over. By way of example, when I realized I was babying my youngest and creating jealousy in the older sibs, I stopped babying her. (Yes, I realize that this can be hard for many parents to do. And, yes, I still baby her here and there.) In the absence of that preferential treatment, I found the space to give my youngest more jobs and more responsibility. Not only did her sisters' moods improve, but more work started getting done around the house. Win-win. I didn't *add* more rules for the older children, and I didn't create punishments. I stopped the dynamic that was hurting my children (and me).

Another habit many parents can immediately stop is the "getting to the bottom" of the fighting. The head of the CIA does less investigating than some of the parents I have worked with! But when the parents stopped trying to uncover every insult, stopped assuming that every sibling squabble was logical, and stopped digging for details, they were left with children who needed support instead of blame and shame. Without trying to apply logic to an emotional problem, things got better! The children still fought here and there, but it became quickly apparent that one child needed the most support, and the parent was able to connect rather than simply discipline. A sea change, really. I had a client, for example, who sent her two boys into the basement to play after school. Even with snacks and everything they needed, they could not handle the close proximity, and the two boys would trade insults and shoves until the mother got involved. She would sit each one on the couch and grill the boys about who had said what, why, and when; who had started the pushing, and who had accelerated it all by throwing the remote. As you can imagine, when the mother stopped her interrogations, it made room for techniques that actually worked. Simple to understand, hard to do.

What Else Can Be Done?

Stopping our own bad parental habits and keeping our mouths shut is an important parenting tool, and I believe you are more than capable of resisting your own bad parenting habits. After zooming out, we can see our added drama and unkindness. I know the difference between fanning the flames of resentment and bringing peace to my own children, and I have seen parents swap out reactions for positive, connective, and simple techniques to promote sibling serenity.

Have a family meeting. The family meeting is the most powerful way to address problems and add connectivity to a family, and bring relief to sibling drama. Depending on how deep the anger and frustration run, the family meeting may take a minute (or months) to help, but the meeting serves as a calm place to air grievances and plan the family's next steps. The younger your children when you start the meetings, the more useful they are and the better your children will get along, but don't despair if you have tweens and teens! It is never too late to begin a family meeting! And while there are many iterations of the family meeting (a quick Google search will yield a long list), the essence of the meeting is this: There is a distinct time and place where you meet, and you use a timer to keep it on track. You can set the rules for the meeting: no name-calling, no calling people out, no overt meanness, no shaming and so forth, but the willingness to adhere to these rules depends on how discouraged your children are. If you are met with crossed arms and rolling eyes, go slowly. Positive communication takes time! You *always* begin the meeting by focusing on the good: what is working, how everyone is adding to the family (especially the most discouraged child), and then you can move on to the problem-solving portion of the meeting. This may feel Pollyannaish, but children need to see you role-model finding the good, even when times are tough. The family meeting takes practice, but your children can learn to communicate their grievances without physically and emotionally attacking each other (most of the time).

Spend special time with each child. Almost 98 percent of the time, the sibling who is struggling the most needs the most encouragement, not the most punishment. It may feel like you are spoiling the "troublemaker," but you simply have to believe that if your child could do better, they would. Pretty powerful, right? If you believe that your child is doing the best they can rather than purposely being a little terror in order to ruin the family, you can move from resentment to empathy. Spending connective time with your child is healing and reaffirming; it tells your child, "Listen, things aren't perfect, but I am always in your corner. I love you and I have your back." There isn't a human on earth who doesn't want to feel that way, and when your child feels like you are on their side, misbehavior goes down. Why? They don't have to work hard or misbehave for your love. They trust that, even when things are bad, you are there for them. This form of connection, while not always yielding the fastest results, plants seeds that grow for years to come. The reason special time helps sibling relationships is simple: When the child feels seen and heard by their caregiver, and when they are allowed to complain and let out their negative feelings, the child is less likely to act on all of their frustrations with their sibling. Special time with a parent acts as a release valve for all the pent-up anger in the child.

If your child could do better, they would.

Have the consequences ready ahead of time. If you are doing drive-by punishments every time your children fight, you are stuck in parenting reactive mode (more on drive-by discipline in Chapter 7). You certainly aren't helping anyone improve their behavior with your reactions, and you most likely feel exhausted and out of control. Setting up the consequences ahead of time ("When you tease your sister about her dolls, you lose TV for the rest of the day" or "When you tease your brother at breakfast, you lose your playdate after school") keeps the dynamics clear, fair, and a bit more impersonal. And an important detail: Do not take away time from you, the parent, as a punishment. Don't cancel book time or the dinner together or a special outing (unless everyone is so angry that the event will become a total mess). Taking yourself away is a major act of war in a small-time skirmish; don't use your relationship as a weapon. If you are wondering about this, reread the "special time" strategy above.

Use the same boat. This is a pretty simple strategy and is a subset of having consequences ready ahead of time. Here's the deal: If one child receives a consequence, all of the sibs get the consequence. This can feel incredibly unfair (and the children will all loudly tell you so), but this is an excellent strategy if all of the children are involved in the drama. It also cuts down on "You never get mad at Katie!" lines. Only use this consequence if all of the children are (mostly) equally at fault, most of the time. If one sibling is suffering and deeply discouraged, the "same boat" consequence will become more *Titanic* than *The Love Boat*, so be on the lookout for how this strategy is affecting the children.

Understand the difference between getting loud and getting mean. Yes, I know, I know. We live in a parenting culture that commands every parent to be utterly calm and in control, yet also be the parent with strong and consistent boundaries. But guess what? Sometimes, for the right parent, raising your voice is what is needed. Yup, you just read that right. If you are the parent who runs for the hills every time your children fight, you must practice using your voice. I am not suggesting you go berserk here, screaming and hollering, foaming at the mouth, and generally acting like a lunatic. No. I am suggesting you get in front of the bathroom mirror and *loudly* say, "THAT'S ENOUGH!" And "STOP IT!" And "SEPARATE, NOW!" And "NO!" If you are wondering how loud to be, go ahead and practice while you are all alone. If you have a smidge of self-awareness, you will know when you are stretching your own boundaries; it will feel uncomfortable and a little scary. And while most of my coaching work is helping parents go from level 10 to 2, I often meet parents who need to practice adding some alarm and volume to their parenting. Yes, adding alarm! We were given voices, and dammit, you are meant to use them (if for no other reason than to break through the noise of your fighting children)! I am not inviting you, I repeat, *not inviting* you to begin yelling at your kids as a way to fix sibling fighting, nor am I also not inviting you to lecture-shout (that's the fastest way to become the *Peanuts*' teacher, "Wah wah

wah . . ."), but I am asking you to step into your parenting power. Stop running from your children when they fight, and speak up. So many parents have been coached to be wishy-washy and whispery and weak, but it is not "positive" or "mindful" or "conscious" parenting to allow your children to rip each other to shreds while you squeak out gentle admonitions or try to coach them on their feelings. Speak up. Be in charge. Your children *need* you to be in the lead and they need to feel your confidence, even if you are faking it until you make it. And once you get their attention, you can then pivot to other strategies.

Adjust your expectations. While not an obvious strategy, there are many parents who simply don't understand the behavior of an average eight-year-old (let alone an eleven-year-old, a six-year-old, and a four-year-old), as well as how children behave when they are smooshed all together, all of the time. Parents tend to think that siblings are either meant to act as feral cats (rolling around, punching each other) or born communicating their innermost emotions and enjoy being around each other 24/7. Both extremes are inaccurate, and you need to discover two things: what is considered typical behavior for any given age, and then what is characteristic for your children. Continuously checking your experience against accepted developmental standards gives you a realistic understanding of what you can expect and which behaviors you can stop under- or over-reacting to! Also, don't compare your three boys to the two girls who live next door (and vice versa). Likewise, don't compare your two children to the five children down the street. Just don't compare, period. When it comes to your children and their battles, it is truly powerful to "know when to hold 'em, know when to fold 'em, know when to walk away, and know when to run." (This is actually good advice for everything in life, thank you, Kenny.)

Keep your sense of humor. Are there stories of extreme bullying among siblings, and do these people grow up to write terrifying memoirs that can make you stay up at night with paranoia? Yes (and BTW, I cannot conceive of a reason one would write a memoir of a happy childhood . . . *boring*). And maybe this bullying is happening in your family. Sure. And if you think that one of your children is singularly targeting their siblings in cruel, repetitive, and terrifying ways, do something about it now. But for the rest of us who have just regular ol' annoying kids who fight, keeping your sense of humor is the difference between unmitigated misery and ordinary annoyance. Once, when trapped in my minivan, my children seemed to have grown octopus arms and were punching each other at angles that seemed physically impossible. Each one of the three children was either screaming, crying, or plotting their revenge, and as soon as I fixed one screaming child, another fight was breaking out. At one point, I pulled over the minivan and started laughing. I turned on "Welcome to the Jungle" by Guns N' Roses and announced, "Have at it, girls!" They were so shocked that I pulled over (as well as by Axl's wailing) that my kids immediately stopped fighting, right in mid-punch. "No," I said, laughing, "get it all out!" My kids sat back, defeated. "Mom, if we stop fighting, will you turn off the music?" The point of this story is that, while humor cannot fix truly hurt feelings and big sibling problems, it can break up the tedium of the same ol' sibling fight. Keep your humor light, non-sarcastic, and not targeted at one child.

Keep them apart *and* keep them together. If this solution sounds like a paradox, that's because it is. For some families, the solution to the bickering and the meanness is clear: The children need time *apart*. Many families I coach are obsessed with doing everything together as a family, and I get it. Most of us are working parents who feel like we hardly see our kids and want quality time whenever we can get it. Fair. But there are times in our children's lives where that is simply not feasible. Why are you going to drag everyone to the diner when one child simply cannot stop bothering his brother? Why are you going to drag the whole family to the movie when one of the children is wildly hormonal and hates everyone? I am not saying that the family ceases to exist as a unit; I just want you to ask yourself: Am I pushing these children together, too much, to satisfy my own needs? *It's okay to separate your children for a while.* Conversely, I have met parents that are so hell-bent on keeping the children separated that the kids don't actually know how to be together; meaning, they haven't been able to tussle, disagree, duke it out, and find some resolution. They haven't built any *sibling resilience.* Are there special cases when children really cannot be together for a certain amount of time? Yes, but generally speaking, we parents have to allow our children to learn how to be together (with our loving and strong guidance). If we Gumby ourselves into making sure each sibling is *happy* and unperturbed, we rob our children of the opportunity to handle the inherent unfairness and struggle that comes with being a sibling and in a family. It is such a good primer for the inequities of daily life, and sibling fights allow opportunities for children to learn when to communicate their needs and when to just walk away. If parents take too many pains to control their children's interactions, it becomes harder and harder for the children to adapt to each other. The confusing part? There will be times in your life where you keep your children apart, and there will be times when the children need to be kept together (and let the adaption occur with some guidance from you). Don't overthink it; just keep zooming out and asking what the needs truly are for your children.

Help the child build skills. Recognize that, for instance, your first child is verbose and communicates every emotion that crosses their mind, but your second child keeps everything close to the chest. This second kid keeps their feelings bottled up until poof! Their frustrations explode all over their siblings. We don't need to make the second child into an extrovert nor do we need to silence the first child, but maybe we can build the needed skills so that each child can slow down and find the right words or actions for a given situation. Figuring out which child needs which skills can feel cumbersome and daunting, but if you begin to analyze the why and the patterns of the sibling fights in your house, the child who needs support could crystallize. Some children need help recognizing how feelings move and feel in their bodies. Some children need to rehearse (over and over) how to let someone know they want to be left alone. Some children struggle with taking turns and need role-modeling, and some take every slight so personally, they need help understanding when an issue is not about them at all. As parents, we may need to ask for help on this front: Therapists, group therapy, coaches, and other specialists are meant to help us with these issues. There is absolutely no reason to go it alone.

Give it a minute. You may have other ideas for how to improve sibling relationships and to that I say: Go for it! As long as the solution has positive and connective roots, I suggest taking a whack at it. Here is the tricky part: Any positive parenting technique needs to be repeated enough to give it a real chance of working, but not used *too* long if it becomes apparent that the suffering is acute. Achieving this middle way (recognizing that you have given a technique a true try) can be unclear, so one idea is to mark on your calendar when you've started using a new strategy so that you have a true sense of how long you have tried it. I have tried solutions over the years only to find myself looking at my husband and asking, "We've been trying to help Gigi get along with her sisters by asking her how she feels . . . It isn't working today, and it didn't work at all this week . . . When did we begin this anyway?" My husband has always shrugged, leaving us unsure of how to proceed (because when a solution isn't working, the brain will assume it will never work and you should quit right away).

And if I have said it once, I have said it a million times: What is medicine now may become poison later. A strategy may work so elegantly and so quickly, it is utterly shocking: *Yes*, you think. *I have found The Answer.* But when you go to use it again, you find that not only does the strategy not work, it is now a disaster! Your children grow and change (so do you), and with this growth comes the need to let go of the old ways. Scary as it will feel, if you keep looking at the patterns in your family, you will find your way.

REFLECT AND WRITE

1. What are the true dynamics of the struggles between your children?

2. Are the struggles happening all of the time or just now and then?

3. Are the dynamics involving all of the children, or are the tiffs related to one child?

4. Is there a transition or dynamic in the family that you've been ignoring, glossing over, or making too much of?

5. Have you been using too many punitive and negative consequences?

6. Do you understand the developmental stages of your children?

7. Do you take the fighting too seriously or not seriously enough?

8. Are you hopping from one strategy to the next, not allowing one to have a chance to work?

9. Are you beating one strategy to death, even though it is obvious it is never going to work?

10. Are you afraid to let your children suffer any consequences?

11. Do you need more support or help with these sibling squabbles?

12. Are you afraid of your children's arguments and violence?

CHAPTER 5

Are You Pushing Your Children to the Proverbial Edge?

You know who Jerry Seinfeld is; you may know him from his Netflix show *Comedians in Cars Getting Coffee*, or his lengthy stand-up career, or his nine-season show, *Seinfeld*. That show was a cultural phenomenon and, if you are a younger parent and have never watched it (what?!), google it. Back then (the olden days of the '90s), just about everyone watched *Seinfeld*. It was a revolutionary show about nothing. There were no typical thirty-minute problems that got resolved by the con-clusion of the show, no true romances, no dramatic issues. The show had a wacky group of friends who sometimes wore puffy shirts and met characters who withheld soup at restaurants (Soup Nazi, anyone?). It was ridiculous, really. Jerry and his costars were mega-famous, their contracts were lucrative, and there was no end in sight. And then in December of 1997, Jerry Seinfeld announced that the current season would be their last season. Why would a comic at the top of his career, the top of his game, quit when he was at the utter peak of success? The answer was simple: He wanted to go out on top. "I wanted to end the show on the same kind of peak we've been doing it on for years," Seinfeld said. "I wanted the end to be from a point of strength. I wanted the end to be graceful."

What the heck does this have to do with parenting?

Well, parents call me or write to me because they are struggling. Something (or many things) is not working in their family and it is my job to understand why they are struggling, help them find their intuition and solutions that may work for their particular situation. I am helping them to "Seinfeld" their situations; find some parenting strength and grace.

Over time, I began to see a surprising trend in parents of both younger and older children alike: I found that the parents were (unintentionally, mind you) pushing their child to their emotional edges in situations that did not demand this level of pushing. I found, over and over, that the parents were not exiting the birthday party, the argument, the playdate "from a point of strength" or in a "graceful" way. And since the parent kept unconsciously yanking their children around, rather than addressing the real needs of the situation (reread Chapter 3, if you need to), the children exhibited horrible behaviors, such as hitting, screaming, running away, name-calling, and defiance, just to name a few. The parents would punish, control, and worry over these behaviors, never realizing that there was a window, a space, a time when the parent had a choice to end the situation "from a point of strength." It is easy for parents to fall victim to this cycle of pushing and explosion and blame, all while never realizing . . . it may have never needed to get so bad to begin with.

Allow me to give you an example, from my own parenting life, of how I ignored my own parenting intuition and pushed my children to the proverbial edge.

When my children were young (seven, four, and one), I would often attend early dinner parties at my dear friend Jen's house. I hope you have a Jen in your life; Jen is the host to all she loves. Everyone would drag their children to her house, the kids would play, the adults would order pizza and chat, and everyone had a *break*. (How long were some of those days with young children? Years? Decades? Centuries? In another space-time continuum, am I still on my hands and knees, sweeping Cheerios off of the floor?) All of the kids mostly got along, and since there would be somewhere between five and ten kids there at any time, it was easy to find a playmate.

One particular outing to Jen's house, I noticed that one of my children (five years old at the time) was a little tired and crabby, but I fed her and got her settled as soon as I arrived at Jen's house. She played happily for a couple of hours, but sometime around 7:00 p.m., she started to circle me, whining, and pulling at my leg. I waved her off, "Go play, Mommy is talking to Jen!" and she would wander off for a couple of minutes, only to return with a slightly louder whine and a more forceful tug on my jeans. There is nothing more grating to my ears than whining, so I found myself fully annoyed and beginning to, ever-so-slightly, push my lovely daughter away from me, using a tone that increased in both threat and anger. I may have begun to whisper-yell, that lovely combo of hissing that parents do when their annoyance is hitting its peak but they don't want to unleash all of the anger in front of their friends.

This wasn't going to go well, was it?

Because boredom and fatigue almost always overtake children's good intentions, my child was soon back at my side. Even though I whisper-yelled in earnest and even though I gave her three more cookies, it didn't matter! My child returned with the whining and the leg grabbing. It was at this point that I picked up my child, rolled my eyes to my friends, and muttered something unkind like, "Looks like

Weezy cannot hang, y'all!" and then huffed and puffed as I left the house. My entire family headed home feeling upset, annoyed, angry, and hopeless. It was a crappy way to end a great night, and I added a nice dose of shame to my five-year-old to boot. Sigh.

Does any of this sound familiar? Sure, I was dragging my kids out of my friend's house, so you could say I was technically in charge of my family, but I would not say I was parenting or leading from a place of strength or grace. I would argue I was only slightly more in control than my kids, which is pretty pathetic. And because I was embarrassed that I was the mom that had to leave (why were everyone else's kids so good and my child was the one that had to whine?), you and I both know that my evening didn't get better from there. Exhausted with anger, bedtime wasn't full of smiles and cuddles. I was in control of myself enough to not make things worse, but my children certainly felt my negative and defeated energy.

Maybe you and your young children are having the whining explosion at birthday parties or family get-togethers. Maybe this behavior shows up at your place of worship or maybe you leave the park with these shenanigans every single time. Maybe there is whining and tantrums in every restaurant or coffee house you frequent.

Maybe you are feeling like you are always the parent who cannot stay at the event. Maybe you feel chronically embarrassed, angry, resentful, trapped, and hopeless. And you have read all of the books! "Ignore the whining!" they say. "You have to simply nip this in the bud!" they say. "Give that child a consequence!" they say. And you listen and obey these books, because you are desperate for the whining to stop, but to no avail. Your children's behavior is not getting better, it is only getting worse, which leads to more desperation and confusion, and so the cycle continues. What a mess.

I frequently see children melting down when they are hauled off to dinner after a long day of after-care at school or sports or other activities. These children have nothing left to give, and whereas you may feel fresh as a daisy, the children cannot access any more maturity or patience. But we are desperate for our children to "go along to get along" (as many of us were taught to do), and so being considerate of our children's feelings feels indulgent to us. For some of us, kindness toward our children can feel like spoiling. The family's routine, plus our reactions to our children's fatigue, leads to chronic disagreement and embarrassment.

So, are you a crappy parent, destined to never be able to bring your child anywhere, for any amount of time? No. Somewhere along the way, we missed our *Seinfeld* moment. We missed the window, the opening, the space to parent "from a point of strength" and grace. There was a moment (or two) where we came to a fork in the road of either making the situation better or worse, and because of our mounting frustration and because we were becoming as emotionally dysregulated as our children, we could not zoom out and see this fork in the road, this choice between grace and weakness.

And when you take two highly reactive people (you and your child), ping-ponging off each other like pinballs, who is going to make the next right, logical decision? Well, honey, it ain't the kid! Like a roller coaster cresting over the peak, the child is only picking up more and more momentum toward feeling (behaving) out of control. If the child is young and/or has any developmental issues such as executive functioning issues, SPD, developmental delays, learning disabilities, or emotional issues, then that child is even more compromised when it comes to finding his rational mind. The cortisol flooding his already immature prefrontal cortex renders him a purely emotional being, hence upping the whining and pestering until finally the child bursts in a volcanic meltdown, careening down the steep rollercoaster drop.

What Is Going on in My Brain?
(AKA: Why Do I Keep Doing This?)

How can we find this space of strength and grace, this opportunity that prevents us from becoming a passenger on the child's roller coaster of anger, blame, and passive-aggression? How can we grab back the reins and apply the brakes on this dynamic that both you and the child detest? How can we see the whining as an invitation to connect with our children rather than fight them?

In order to find the space of strength and grace, that moment to make another choice, you need to be willing to look beyond your behavioral habits and objectively see the dynamics of these tussles. If you try to control yourself *and* your child in the moment of anger, you will almost certainly fail. Why? The brain does *not* work like that! When the brain becomes stressed and, this is really important, *when you are not conscious of what the stressor is*, your brain wants to do roughly three things: run like hell, shut down and pretend you're dead and/ or invisible, or fight back with a vengeance. If you are really lucky, your brain can vacillate between all three, making you feel completely out of control! Wheeee!

And for good or bad, our brains are largely still the same brains that the cavemen were using when they were bashing rocks in caves and scanning the plains for food and danger. Our brains are in the business of keeping us safe, and even though our children are not mountain lions, our brains think they are actually keeping us safe from the threat (the screaming child) by running away, playing dead, or fighting back. Add to this panicky brain our genetics, our early childhood experiences, and how functional or dysfunctional our families of origin were (are), and we are left with a soupy mess of reactions to our children's whining.

To sum it up: We cannot completely rely on our brains to help us in the moment of stress and upset when dealing with our kiddos. No, our neural pathways, the ones that keep reacting in anger and control when our children whine, are deeply ingrained. We have some serious grooves going in the brain, and when our stress reaches a certain level, those grooves unconsciously take over. Like our children, we cannot remember our good intentions in the moment of upset. We are like that great TV show that doesn't end in strength or grace; instead, we rumble toward mediocrity or, worse, a train wreck no one wants to watch.

So, let's take a moment. Breathe in and breathe out. If I ask you once, I will ask you a hundred times to breathe. A good, deep belly breath tells our nervous system, "Everything is okay. Please don't panic." Breathing, while not actually fixing the reality of the whining child in front of us, does calm down our jangly nerves and that is half the battle!

Stay curious about the larger dynamic: In a calm, quiet moment, you are going to consider your "Jen's House" moment or event and ask yourself, "Can I see the moment when I lose my leadership? Do I see what is actually happening in this kerfuffle?" Write down what you see. Make it real. Take what you see out of your mind and put it on paper or screen. Yes, eventually you will get so good at catching your reaction that you won't have to write everything down all of the time, but for now? Give your brain some help and move the interior to the exterior. (Again, this is why therapy works. You shift the inside to the outside.)

Here is an example of questions and observations I came up with when I looked at what happened at Jen's house. Let's see if you relate to some of these observations with your own family:

First of all, my daughter was tired when we arrived at the house, and you don't need to be a rocket scientist to admit that everything was going to go wrong sooner rather than later when a five-year-old is tired. Second, she had already played with kids for a couple of hours after arriving and, at five years of age, what else did I want from her? I had a bit of developmental disconnect. As for another developmental fumble, whining is not developmentally out of line for a child her age. I mean, did I expect her to say (put on a good British accent), "Ahem, dearest Mother . . . I do believe that I am, in fact, overwhelmed and simply exhausted by this long day. My fellow playmates are a bit brutish and annoying, and I would very much like to go home. Thank you for your consideration." Nope, at five she doesn't have many mature communication tools in her toolbox, and I was unreasonable to expect anything other than whining. In fact, whining was a pretty good start. Third, continuously pushing my child away as well as blowing off her needs was, maybe (just maybe), not an effective way to placate any human, let alone a five-year-old. I have yet to meet a person who enjoys feeling ignored and, worse, completely dismissed (insert facepalm here). In fact, when we dismiss a needy human, two things happen: They either increase their neediness with a vengeance or they give up, no longer placing their needs and desires out there for anyone to satisfy. And yes, while a needless child sounds dreamy, children are *meant* to trust the adults in their lives to help, support, and listen to them. If a child learns, early on, that their main attachments will never listen to them, the child will turn inward. This is not confidence; this is a shutdown and you don't want that. And finally, a crystal-clear takeaway from this messy meltdown was my need for a personal break. I badly wanted to see my friends, laugh with them, and simply *be*, unencumbered by responsibility and mothering duties. I didn't want anyone to ask me for anything and I didn't want to take care of anyone. When I got honest with myself and listened to my intuition in this zoom out, I knew I wanted to be free of my children for a couple of hours. I know you understand the urge.

Needless to say, this serious fatigue and burnout wasn't helping in the compassion department when it came to parenting with strength and grace. (And I think this exhaustion is a major cause of many of our parenting meltdowns, FYI.)

How Can You Find More Space and Grace
(AKA: Stop Bullshitting Yourself)?

Let's take a look at your life, at the areas that may require more attention, and find some simple ways to get ahead of the drama. You can be more proactive than reactive, so let's take a peek at how you can avoid pushing your child to the absolute edge, too often.

1.   As best as you can, assess the fatigue level of your children before entering a situation. It may not change the reality of going to the event or place, but at least it is a real-time estimate of the possible challenges you are facing when it comes to your children. (This advice goes for you parents of teens, too).

2.   What can you actually expect from your children, developmentally speaking, in this given scenario? This is not about charts you are reading in a book or online. I am not talking about wishful thinking or what you think should be happening. No, this is about the reality of your children, as you know them here and now. What can they actually handle?

3.   Which behaviors are a sign that parental compassion, empathy, and presence are needed, and fast? When we parents begin to slow down and pay attention, our children

are often telling us exactly what they need! They will say, outright, "I am tired" or "I am hungry" or "I am bored." Maybe these are red herrings for other needs, but your child is still trying to tell you something and it is always worth listening.

4.   What else can you do when your child needs your attention? After decades of working with children and families, studying my bottom off, and working with some of the best professionals out there, I have a ton of tools in my toolbox, but guess what? I wasn't born with all of them, and chances are good, neither were you. I want this book to be your opening to putting all options on the table (except, of course, physical and emotional abuse). Giving in to your children's needs in a certain scenario? On the table. Ignoring the whining? On the table. Offering a reward for listening and following instructions? On the table. Creating boundaries and consequences? On the table. When you begin to open your mind to other ideas, you will be surprised how you have limited yourself in your parenting choices. You have probably been in a self-imposed parenting prison of theories and trends, of "always's" and "never's," so let's break out.

5.   Are you trying to do too much all at once? Were you trying to have fun with your friends *and* feed the kids dinner *and* expect them to hang out with each other *and* expect it all to go smoothly? Are you trying to get young children to sit quietly at church while you volunteer and take care of your aging mother? Yes, yes, yes, and yes? This is not realistic nor is it fair to anyone in this scenario. I am not blaming

anyone for having desires or hopes, but we cannot have it all, all at the same time. Being an adult and a kind parent means having to accept this hard truth and make the best decision that you can, over and over and over.

Now that you have your little cheat sheet, here is a list of options that can often decrease whining and increase cooperation. Remember: No strategy works 100 percent of the time, and almost all strategies stop working at some point. Finding a parenting technique that works with *your* family requires you to understand yourself, your children, and the needs of the situation. If you are unclear in these understandings, please pause to thoughtfully see the patterns in front of you. As for what you can do to prevent your child's meltdowns . . . ?

Make a plan. You may enjoy "playing everything by ear" or "seeing how it goes" or hoping against hope, but children thrive when there is a plan. Your plan doesn't need to be rigid or have military-precision detail, and your plan can change here and there, but all things being equal, your children still need a plan. The younger and/ or more intense the child, the more a plan is needed. A clear plan makes every human feel safe, and even if your free-spirited self does not enjoy making and keeping a plan, you are doing this for your children and your own sanity.

Get down to your children's level, and I mean literally. Get physically down to their eye level. When your child is bothering you, stop what you are doing, bend down, and listen to them. Now, I will admit to being a "holler from one room to another" kind of parent, but I made a promise to myself to look my children in the eye when they needed something from me, and it has changed everything. When a child feels seen and heard (a deep need for every human), the whining and leg pulling will often abate. It also offers a moment to truly understand what it is that your child needs. It doesn't mean you will drop everything or interrupt your friend mid-thought, but it does mean that you are going to commit yourself to respectfully look your child in the eye when you speak with them. Even if your child is taller than you, take a moment to make proper eye contact, and try to relax your eyes. Your children immediately see your, "Good God, what the hell do you want now, kid?" eyes, so take a deep breath and pretend you are looking at a kitten. Sounds ridiculous, but it works. No one yells at a meowing kitten.

Commit to taking your child into another room (away from the eyes of fellow children and parents), if you need to speak to them/deliver some tough news. Whisper-yelling or outright fighting in front of your friends and family is humiliating for your child and embarrassing for you, and it will only serve to make your blood pressure go up and your compassion go down. You will not be your best self, and you are more likely to overreact when there is an audience. Consciously or unconsciously, you may feel pressured to please or satisfy someone else that you are "tough" or "kind," and that's no way to be with your child. Some privacy takes that pressure off.

Admit to friends and family, ahead of time, that you may need to leave early to preserve some strength and grace in your family. In fact, this can be part of your plan *with* your child. It is perfectly human to have periods in your parenting life where you ask for others' compassion, and trying to not drag out your child's misery is one of them. While you may feel annoyed that you cannot do what you want, when you want, I promise that leaving early is far better than dragging out the pushing and pulling and threatening and anger. You may also be surprised at how supportive your family and friends can be when it comes to you letting them know the deal. And if they judge you? Well, screw them.

Acknowledge the triggers and automatic thoughts that seem to control your behavior. I laughed out loud when I typed that sub-heading. People spend *their entire* lives finding and working with these triggers and I just sub-headed like, "no bigs." It is huge, but don't make a big deal of it. Just ask yourself, "What are some of the realizations that you have when you reflect back on this stressful moment? What are your chronic triggers, thoughts, and feelings?" With honest reflection, we can begin to change how we react to our unconscious minds, and we can stop beating up ourselves and our children and begin to behave with more strength and grace. You can absolutely condition yourself to see your thinking coming down the street and decide to cross the block. Again, it won't be perfect and you will make lots of mistakes, but if you slow down enough to see your patterns of thoughts *and choose another plan*, you can make huge headway in bringing more space and grace to your children.

But What About . . .

Now it is time for some FAQs for handling or leaving a situation with strength and grace:

But, Meghan, we are at an event for one of my children (a piano recital) and we just cannot leave! What am I supposed to do for my four-year-old who won't stop whining?

Yup, I hear you. You have paid for the lessons and you have endured listening to Chopin's Prelude in E Minor, Opus 28, No. 4 over and over.

So what can you do? Nowhere in this chapter have I said that children may not cry or be upset, nor will I ignore that sometimes a parent's gotta do what a parent's gotta do. For instance, strength and grace may look like packing a big bag of toys (and yes, technology) and snacks so that you can have an arsenal of options for when the going gets tough. Strength and grace may look like waiting until your child plays their piano piece, and then stepping out into the hall with your squirmy four-year-old. Would it appear more polite to watch all seven hundred children play "Für Elise"? Yes, but that just may not be in the cards. I have even been known to hand my smartphone to a complete stranger so that she can film my child play her piece while I stepped outside to allow my other child to have her fit. And not one parent has judged me, said no, or has been anything other than kind. They've either been in the same predicament or they are wise enough to know they will be soon enough.

But, Meghan, you expect me to parent with strength and grace and prevent every single meltdown that comes my way?

Good God, no. What are you, a robot? If you could prevent meltdowns all of the time, then you should be writing this book and selling out stadiums. No. Until the end of time, children will melt down. In fact, they are designed to melt down; it is how they mature. Having life not go their way (and adapt to this) is the work of a child, hence the tears and tantrums and some violence. It sucks, but it is the truth.

In no way am I suggesting that, when you parent with strength and grace, you will control your children's emotions. Going out like Seinfeld is about you. It is about taking responsibility for yourself, your big emotions, and your automatic thoughts. The hope is (and my coaching has shown this to be true) that the more responsibility you take for yourself, the more clearly you see your children and the more you can parent proactively. So, go ahead and expect that your child will test you until the end of time. That is okay; that's life. Just know that there are better ways to handle these tests.

> The more responsibility you take for yourself, the more clearly you see your children and the more you can parent proactively.

But, Meghan, giving my child strong eye contact and listening to him every single time he whines will only increase the whining, right?

Yes and no. So, let's clear something up: Listening to your child, showing empathy and compassion, and finding solutions with your child does not spoil them. Showing kindness and warmth does not create a brat. What creates a brat? Chronic back and forth, parental indecision, and allowing the child to take the lead of how the events unfold . . . *Those* patterns create a brat.

True, the child may be upset and tired and spent, and these realities may lead to you all leaving a party, and that may cause you to *feel* like you are capitulating, but you are the one actually calling the shots, not the child. If you stay self-possessed, positive, and clear-headed, the child will feel like you are in charge, and even though the situation isn't ideal, the child isn't the boss of you! But if the child is talking you in and out of decisions and pushing you around, this is what leads to bratty behavior. It is a small but discernible difference, this reacting versus responding. Staying in parenting reaction mode is unconscious, fear-based, and seems to make no one happy. Having a *response* is the measured acknowledgment of the reality in front of you. Response takes real factors into account and is not laden with explosive emotions. Again, I am not suggesting that responding is easy, but the strength and grace in it will save your parenting life.

Again, listening to a child does not spoil them.

But, Meghan, I have really worked on this and feel completely out of control. I don't feel or see my intuition kicking in; if anything, my explosiveness is growing, my anger is seething, and I am getting more and more frustrated.

If you challenge yourself to change and be better, and you are running into depression, anger, and anxiety, you need support. If you dive into the deep end of your psyche alone and only continue to suffer without a whiff of emotional growth, you will feel like you are spiraling, drowning, or drifting away, and no one wants that (especially your family). Many of us are carrying trauma that we simply packed away, long ago, to simply survive our day-to-day lives. That trauma is just sitting there, largely unchanged and often made worse by time and avoidance. Many of us have spent decades peeking at the pain and shutting that door, and why? That level of pain feels like too much. But, depending on what happened to you, how old you were, and how alone you were in facing it, this trauma is now like a cancer. It creeps and seeps and infects all parts of your life, preventing joy and even preventing proper sorrow. You owe it to yourself to take a peek under the hood and take care of yourself. Scary? Sure, but might as well suffer in service for change, rather than suffer for the sake of suffering.

So, if you are finding deep resistance to change, if you are exceptionally and indiscriminately panicked and angry, and if you feel hopeless, please find someone to help you. And because therapy is an intense relationship, you get to choose someone you click with. You are allowed to sample and try numerous therapists, you are allowed to begin therapy and then quit to find another person, and you are allowed to question the therapist with whom you work. You are the customer, and they are offering you a service, so be sure it works for you.

As Anne Lamott says, "My mind is a neighborhood I try not to go into alone." Find your person to help you walk into your mind, so you can live your life with more strength and grace.

REFLECT AND WRITE

1. Do I have reasonable developmental expectations of my children? Is there an extra need or consideration paid for my intense child that I am ignoring or hoping will just go away?

2. Do I have a plan when I leave the house and do I execute said plan? Don't worry, you probably won't always have a twenty-four-point checklist to manage, but you may need one for now.

3. Have I set up my children for success? For example, have I provided them with a schedule, let them know who will be there, and had them gather some toys and snacks for themselves?

4. Is there another way to attend events that don't *always* include my family?

5. Am I willing to relax my rules to get through an event? Candy and technology come to mind . . .

6. Do I understand that I am gaslighting my children by pushing them past their limits and then blaming them for melting down?

7. Am I willing to let go of the parenting trends or theories that I adopted to "fix" my whining kids? Are the theories making everything worse?

CHAPTER 6

When You Are Falling Out of the Pose, Look Like You Meant to Do It

I love yoga, and I am lucky to have had (and currently have) some amazing teachers. Each is so different and I am endlessly impressed with their knowledge, compassion, and practice. One such teacher is Lily. Lily is in her sixties and has a no-nonsense approach to her yoga. She won't use the Sanskrit terms and explicitly teaches physiology, demanding each student obey their own bodies. And in every class, she inevitably announces, "Time for balancing!" and everyone collectively groans. Of course, no one wants to balance! Flowing, twisting, *anything* other than balancing is preferred. And trust me, Lily knows why we are miserable: The more you try to control the balance, the more you topple over, but if you don't focus at all, you will become distracted and fall over. It can be challenging for even the most practiced yogi, and it is easy to feel resistant.

One day, Lily announced, "Time for balancing," and everyone reluctantly readied themselves. As we began to slowly lift one leg to balance on the other, she said, "Listen, you are going to fall out of the pose. It's okay. Just look like you meant to do it. I mean, you can feel yourself losing your balance, so don't fight it. Lose your balance and make it look like it was on purpose."

I literally stopped in my balancing tracks and looked straight at her. Wow. That was some parenting dharma right there! And I love a metaphor and will beat it to death, but this was no metaphor. *Looking like you meant to fall out of balance when you begin to lose the balance is a powerful parenting move.* Would it be preferable to always know what problems are coming down the pike with our kids? Yes! Would I prefer that all parents feel confident and sure-footed all of the time? Yes! Is that reasonable? No, not even close to reasonable. Sure, sure . . . if you have parented more than five minutes, you probably know when your little one is too tired and overwhelmed; you have *some* knowledge of your child's basic needs and how these needs mess with their behaviors. But children, especially as they get older, have their own interior worlds. They have their own desires, opinions, and stories in their minds. They themselves are chronically falling out of balance due to their immaturity; in fact, the very essence of being a child is going in and out of balance. And while it would be lovely to expect you to always keep your regulation, that's just not reasonable. We are human. The difference between us adults and the kids is that we have the power to step out of ourselves, catch ourselves as we fall, and *choose another path.*

What are the reactions to feeling like we are losing our parenting equilibrium (similar to losing our balance)?

1.   **Outright anger and blame.** When this parent feels out of control, the child is the nail and the parent is the

hammer. "It is my child's fault that I feel out of control. If he just listened to me, I wouldn't feel so out of control. He pushes all my buttons, and he knows he is doing it."

2.   **Passive-aggression.** This parent may be seething with anger, but she is smiling through gritted teeth. This parent may also sigh, roll eyes, give up, and give in to the child's demands the more she feels pushed around and out of control.

3.   **Calm purpose.** Many parents react to the loss of control with equanimity, focus, and relaxation. I am not often enough that parent, myself, but these parents have trained their limbic systems to not react with sheer panic when they feel out of control or lost. Some people are more naturally relaxed, but most parents have found a way to react with calm purpose by practicing it.

Not sure how *you* react to feeling out of control with your children? Let's use the example of your child begging for ice cream after school to see where you may fall:

So, the ice-cream truck pulls up to the school every day at 3:10 p.m. and blasts its horrible music, alerting everyone within a ten-block radius that it is there, thankyouverymuch. And let's say you say no, pretty much every time the child asks. Why? First of all, those Popsicles are hella overpriced; second, it's too much sugar; and third, the line is too long and you have people to see and stuff to do. Despite your constant no's, your child still responds to the siren song of the ice-cream truck with plaintive pleas, promises, and negotiations that would make a DC lawyer proud. And like a smack to the head, you suddenly realize you are kind of being a control freak about this whole Popsicle thing. The kid wants a SpongeBob Popsicle, not co-caine, for chrissakes. As you realize you have been a bit rigid, you can feel yourself losing your parenting balance, right there about twenty feet from the ice-cream truck. Your mind begins to spin. What are you supposed to do, just give in to your child's begging, tears, ha-rassment, and haranguing? Just abandon all of your rules and bound-aries? Won't you look weak? Won't your child lose respect for you? Won't you create a nightmare? Won't you have to buy your child a Popsicle every single day for the rest of his life?

And in case you think this Popsicle example is "no big deal," our parenting lives are literally created by a million little moments exactly like this. It is the accumulation of "Popsicle decisions" that create the tapestry and story of our parenting lives. This Popsicle moment is also about when your kid asks to go on birth control or they beg to charge their phones in their rooms or you find weed in their drawer or they declare they are no longer attending church with the family or they dinged the front of the car in the drive-through lane. How you handle the Popsicle situation is how you handle your parenting life, make no mistake.

So, let's apply the three reactions (anger, passive-aggression, and calm purpose) to the Popsicle debacle.

If you jump straight to anger and blame, your child begins to beg for the treat and there is a quiet voice whispering that you have gone too far in your no's. You know you are being ridiculously rigid, and even though you know you have taken this boundary too far and even though every single one of your child's friends is lined up, as you waver and lose your balance, your brain panics and doubles down. "I said no. No ice cream. Not now, not ever." This happens so quickly, you may not even be aware that it is happening. To put the cherry on this sundae, you blame your child for your guilt. "If you didn't whine every time, maybe I would get you your ice cream, but now the answer is no." It is a mess. Remember, you fell out of balance because you had an intuition that you were *not making the right choice*. There was some kind of cognitive dissonance, a whiff of "wait a second, what am I doing here and why?" Anger flies out of your mouth because to admit that you are wrong, to say, "I have misjudged this," is extraordinarily vulnerable to the brain. The brain doesn't like to feel unsafe. It feels better to be angry than vulnerable. It sucks to parent like this. If you are an angry parent, you are likely a tired parent.

If you are passive-aggressive, you may sputter out a "Fine, just please stop whining. We can get a Popsicle this once, but never ever again, okay?" Include loud sighs and a pinched face that appears to be trying to smile, and you are the picture of quiet resentment. The passive-aggressive parent wants to simultaneously give in and hold the boundary and stop the whining, and these interior conflicts create a great deal of tension. The sighing, playing the victim, and the indecisiveness are toxic for the child, assuredly, but they are truly painful for the psychological life of the parent. Unlike the outwardly angry parent, the passive-aggressive parent is feeling the volcanic anger but they stuff it all down, keeping all of their doubt and anger inside. The child can feel this confusion roiling in the parent, but they don't know what to make of it.

You may imagine that the parent who "falls out of the pose with calm purpose" is like a unicorn, not even real. But believe me, we are surrounded by these parents! It is not as though these parents don't become flustered or indecisive or confused; *they just don't react to their wobbles with anger or passive-aggressiveness.* Or rather, they catch themselves before they allow their limbic systems to lose it. The parent who is losing patience with the whining child at the ice-cream truck may respond with something like, "You know what? I have changed my mind. It is hot, I would like to buy you a Popsicle, and I would like one, too! What do you think I should get?" Voilà! Rather than react to vulnerability, fear, and panic, this parent has gracefully owned exactly what was happening and made it into something fun and easy. Their thinking goes like this: "Wait, I have gone too far with this Popsicle thing. I feel unsure, the child can see that I am waffling, and I don't want to lose my authority. How do I lean into this with kindness and discipline?"

You may think you cannot do that, and that reacting to your parenting fears with "calm purpose" is out of your reach. You may think that you don't have control over your emotions enough to fall out of balance with purpose, control, and kindness. You may think I, Meghan, have been doing this calm purpose routine from the very start and I now sit here, all yogi-smug, voice oozing in a meditative drone, "Just simply realize you have lost your way and exit that frustration, easily and seamlessly."

No. Not even close.

As I have mentioned above, I am a (former) angry person. Back in my youth, when I felt even mildly threatened, I would "act *then* think," and if anyone had told me that I could choose *not* to react to my jacked-up nervous system, I would have called them a liar (actually, I would have called them a "FUCKING LIAR" because I was a potty-mouthed angry person). I got into fistfights (have you seen my crooked nose on Insta?), sassed my peers and adults alike, and generally pretended I didn't care about a thing. So, if anyone is susceptible to snapping at their children or being passive-aggressive, it's me. I don't think my Buddha nature is angry and violent, but undoing my anger and learning how to fall out of balance gracefully was not easy. Still isn't. Fatigue, hunger, hormones, my DVR not recording *The Real Housewives of Atlanta* . . . anything can throw me off my game. Same as you, right? It is called being human. But if I didn't believe I could change and *be better*, what is the point of this life? Not that I had to change every aspect of myself, but could I ask myself to react with calm purpose, at least some of the time? Could I let go of my rigidity and my ego and my stories? Could I expect myself to be more mature than my own children? Can you?

Falling out of parenting balance with calm purpose can offer you many gifts, and here are a few:

It gives you a moment to reset and pivot (yes, a couple of seconds is a moment). Pivot toward what, you ask? Toward *anything* positive! As a parent you can pivot toward saying yes (which is awesome, especially if you are a control freak). It can also help you pivot toward giving a strong "no" (if you happen to get pushed around by your children too often). By way of example, let's flip the Popsicle story. Let's say that every single day, the ice-cream truck parks in front of the school and plays its devious little ditty. And every day, you feel entrapped and browbeaten into purchasing your dear child a Popsicle. One day, you realize that enough is enough. You are running late to an appointment and line-standing is simply not feasible; deep down you also know that you have spent your retirement on ice cream and your child is now addicted to SpongeBob Popsicles, and the worst? Your child is the boss of you. You could revert to the same bad options I mentioned above (outright anger or passive-aggressiveness) or you could come out of the pose gracefully. "Buddy, we always get a Popsicle and today we cannot. I know this is disappointing; you can be upset. We have to go to the doctor. Let's go." Will there be screaming and tantrums? Yes! But better that comes from the kid than you! I am not saying that pivoting out of your imbalance will be easy and work seamlessly every time, but it is your best option. It is a pivot toward positive parental leadership. Think of it like an oxygen mask for anger; you gotta save yourself first.

It allows you to feel compassion toward yourself. When I am wobbling and wiggling and teetering and about to fall in yoga, it is easy to tell myself what a loser I am and think, *Why the hell can't I* *get this right?* Instead, over time I began to see that some days are balance days and some days aren't, and that's okay. I began to see that I will inevitably fall out of a pose, just like it is inevitable that I will lose my way in my parenting life. There will be moment after moment when I don't know what I am doing, and I can *choose* to run around like a chicken with my head cut off or I can decide to calm the eff down a bit. Feeling unsure is not a sign of weakness; feeling unsure is a sign you are parenting.

Feeling unsure is a sign you are parenting.

Losing your parenting balance with grace is quietly powerful. It's not about *if* you will lose your parenting way, it's about how you handle it *when* you do. I have had epic arguments with my teen where she has retreated to her room, doors a-slamming. I have stood outside her door, hand on the doorknob. "I am going to go in and give her a piece of my mind." "I am going to show her who is boss." "She cannot just sit in there . . ." I have felt myself losing my way. Angry Meghan had the right to go in there, but Calm Purpose Meghan just stood there. I didn't know what the hell to do or think, but I knew that what I *didn't do* mattered a great deal. I knew that it mattered that I didn't do harm; I knew it mattered to come out of the wobble with grace and peace. To let the arguing stop. To not be "right," angry, or passive-aggressive. I admit, "calm purpose" is not exciting or even satisfying work. Standing outside a child's room, sweating, unsure, and angry isn't the strategy you will read in a parenting book. This is not an approach that is filled with fancy technique, skill, and fireworks. Falling out of balance with grace and calm purpose is often quiet and simple and hard as hell to do; it doesn't attract too much attention. It is powerful, but not in the way that you might think.

How do you do this? How do you break yourself from chronic re-action? Here are some ideas; see what speaks to you:

1. **Think of a time when you knew you were taking a boundary or rule too far.** Think of a time when you *knew*, in your gut, that you were acting like a lunatic, but you couldn't seem to stop yourself. (If you cannot think of one single time, you are a superhero.) Remember how it felt. Maybe you were ashamed. Maybe you were embarrassed. Maybe you were sad or disappointed in yourself.

2. **Take that incident and zero in on the place where you began to lose your parenting way.** Where did you begin to wobble? When were you grasping? Do you remember any of your automatic thoughts? Thoughts like, *I'm too tired to deal with this*, or *Nothing I do works*, or *If I allow this, everything will go to pot*. Try to remember the thoughts or feelings associated with losing your balance. No judgment here. Just see that place in your mind's eye.

3. **Imagine what it might have looked like to react to yourself and your child with calm purpose.** Maybe you would have gotten down and looked at your child, eye to eye. Maybe you would have listened more and talked less. Maybe you would have smiled and said, "I see where you are coming from!" Maybe you would have laughed instead of attacked. Maybe you would have said, "I know what we are doing!" and then proceeded onward. Maybe you would have been gentle with your voice. Maybe you would have stayed

quiet. Maybe you would have given your one and only "no," and withstood the tantrum. So, close your eyes and play out the scene. You are beginning to lose it, you are beginning to wobble . . . and instead you use calm purpose. What does *that* look like? It doesn't matter if you think you can do it in real life. It doesn't matter if you think your child is too spoiled and wouldn't respond to it. Close your eyes and imagine the scene playing out. And if you want, imagine it playing out in many different peaceful ways . . . There are many ways to apply calm purpose to your parenting.

4.   **Write down how it *felt* to possess this calm purpose.** Any feeling is valid. Scary, exciting, strong, inspiring, shocking, any or all feelings work. Now, write down this sentence stem:

When my child _____,
I usually feel _____, and I react by
_____.
Instead of reacting, I am going to respond by
_____,
And I will feel _____, no matter what happens.

Examples
When my child whines about not wanting to go to school, I usually feel annoyed and angry, and I react by lecturing her on how she needs to go. Instead of reacting, I am going to respond by stopping, getting on my knee, and listening, and I will feel empathy for her, no matter what happens.

When my child refuses to pick up his toys, I usually feel
disrespected and defeated, and I react by doing it for
him because I am too tired to fight. Instead of reacting,
I am going to respond by making a game out of putting
them away, smiling, and having fun with my son, and I
will feel confident this is a better way, no matter what
happens.

When my child hits her brother, I usually feel defensive
and want to punish her, and I react by sending her to her
room. Instead of reacting, I am going to respond by
making sure her little brother is okay and then sit on the
couch with my daughter until she has calmed down, and I
will feel calm, no matter what happens.

Feel free to adjust the script any way you like. You are running
mini rehearsals in your mind of how you can actually change. The
point of this exercise is that you see yourself falling out of balance,
take responsibility for how you respond, and then reimagine the scenario. It is powerful to zoom out and see yourself as a character in
your own Kabuki theater. It is powerful to see that you have a choice
and that you are actually the mature one in the relationship. It is
powerful to acknowledge that how you lose balance is something that
you can mindfully control. You are not beholden to your reactions.
You can choose to respond, you just gotta slow down a little . . . give
your brain a hot minute. It is a panicky organ, this brain of ours, and
despite the fact that it is the most complex organ we have, it is simple
in its desire to keep us safe from harm and perceived danger. So, let's
use that prefrontal cortex of yours and say, "Hey! That's enough outta
you. I am in charge here . . ." I swear, it works. Remember Angry
Meghan? If I can do it, so can you.

Bonus Tip: Want to make this exercise even more powerful? Practice what you would say differently out loud in the mirror to yourself. Practice a calm face, a small smile, and kind eyes. This may feel ridiculous, but do you know what happens to your brain when you smile? Your brain releases neurotransmitters such as dopamine, endorphins, and serotonin (all powerful and good), brain chemicals that aid in calming your nervous system by lowering heart rate and blood pressure. I mean, that's real science, people! And did you know that smiling activates mirror neurons? These cool neurons in our brains mimic what the other person is doing! You smile, mirror neurons light up in your child and *they* smile, unconsciously. It is magic, really. You don't need to memorize complex scripts of what to say to maintain calm purpose or to choose another way.

This activity isn't going to fix you, but reflecting on what isn't working and choosing another way is growth. *That* is a way to find your way through this parenting life. Don't allow the wobbles and worries to paralyze or anger you (at least, not all the time).

And here's a little secret: This works for almost every relationship in your life! Yes, parenting immature people like children can push every seen and unseen button in you, but simply living with other humans can do that, too. Go ahead and use this exercise as you see fit for all of your interpersonal relationships. You will be surprised to see what happens!

Caveat: You may truly realize, through the activity, that you cannot access any feelings. Your neural pathways may be so ingrained in negativity, in feeling threatened, in feeling afraid and angry, that the prospect of responding any other way just feels ridiculously out of reach.

This is good feedback.

You can only move forward from where you are. You cannot skip ahead, and you cannot sit and wish you were different. (I mean, you *can* sit and wish you were different. I do this all of the time, but it won't result in any changes and, in fact, just makes you feel shittier.) You are who you are, where you are, and this is your reality, right now. This is true for all of us. But what is also true for all of us is that the brain is ever-changing and ever able to adapt. We are not static-brained adults, as science of old had us believe. We are able to change how we respond to the world and, most important, our children. You can find examples of this everywhere, from parents who stop spanking to parents who stop chronically yelling and shaming to parents who respond with calm purpose instead of violence or despair. I have seen these changes in the parents I coach, and I have experienced it myself. But for some of us (cough, cough), this is not an easy path. Between my twin besties, depression and anxiety, and my predilection for anger and explosiveness, finding calm purpose and staying positive is a full-time job.

But here is the truthiest truth I can give you: The more I practice losing my balance with equanimity and compassion for myself, the kinder I am toward every sentient being in this world. Most important, my family. Practice makes progress.

Get thee to a therapist if you are stuck. It *will* help (if you find the right therapist).

You are up to the challenge because you picked up this book; it means you care.

REFLECT AND WRITE

1. When you lose your balance, do you respond with anger? Passive-aggression? Both?

2. How did your family of origin respond to uncertainty? How did this affect you growing up? How does it affect you today?

3. After completing the fill-in-the-blank activity, what did you learn about yourself? Your child? Are you panicked that your child will become a monster if you add some flexibility to your parenting life?

4. Does it feel good to know that you don't always have to say no or always say yes to your child? Does it feel good to have choices? Calm purpose doesn't have limits.

5. Does this chapter make you want to take yoga? As in all things: Find a good teacher. No good teacher = no good yoga.

CHAPTER 7

Drive-By Parenting Feels Good and Completely Works . . . Until It Doesn't

When you have a baby, everything is react, react, react. She cries, you react by picking her up. He squeaks, you react by smiling at him. She gives a gummy smile, you really react by acting like a smiling fool yourself! He tries to crawl up the steps, grab the cord, eat the bleach . . . you stop, stop, stop. You aren't even thinking about this reaction; it is 100 percent instinctive and intuitive. If your parenting is in good working order, biology has prepared you to take care of this baby, no matter how flawed and messy you may feel. And this level of care-taking? It is 99.99999 percent reaction on your part.

And then, around toddlerhood, something happens. You are still reacting (you have to; the child is on a death mission even under your constant surveillance), but now your sweet child is meeting you with some defiance. Where you would once scoop up the baby and distract easily, the child now fights you, tooth and nail. Your sweet one's will-power is shocking, but you forge ahead with your reaction, reaction, reaction. You persist in your reaction because you have been told that consistency is the parenting gold standard, and even though your re-actions are becoming increasingly ineffective, what else can you do? This child needs to learn who is boss, and come hell or high water, it is you.

So, you make it through toddlerhood, dazed, exhausted, and slightly traumatized, but you now find yourself in a whole new world of trouble.

You are stuck in drive-by parenting.

Wait, what does this mean? "Drive-by parenting" means that you now walk by your beloved child and fire off dozens of commands and demands, barely even pausing to look in his general direction. In order to beat your child to the punch of bossing *you* around, you don't allow him to make a peep before you fire off enough orders to make a marine drill sergeant proud. With the child barely out of diapers, you find yourself becoming the parent you never imagined you would be: a complete and total nag.

"Stop touching that."

"Help your sister."

"Get off the couch."

"Pick up your toys."

"Where is your backpack?"

"Go to the bathroom."

"Go to bed."

"Go to your room."

"Get your shoes."

"Get your lunch."

"Get off the iPad."

"Get off the iPad."

"Get off the iPad."

"Did you hear me?"

"Did you hear me?"

"Did you hear me?!?!"

And those mandates and directives have come in just the first hour of the day! If you awaken by 6:00 a.m., you have probably bossed your child around at least twenty times by 7:00 a.m. Do you think I am kidding? Put down this book (temporarily) or use the margin of the page to stop, reflect, and jot down all of the commands you have given today alone. And what happens when we make constant demands on and commands to our children, especially when we are in a hurry? Well, you tell me! Check the boxes that apply to your parenting life (and these are not "here and there" parenting examples; these are chronic parenting problems cropping up in your family on a daily basis):

❏   Your child ignores you completely when you try to tell him to do almost anything.

❏   You are punishing your child daily for "not listening" (and there is no evidence of any serious executive functioning or any other attention-related issues in the child).

❏   Your child is beginning to do or already does the opposite of what you have asked him to do.

❏   You dread every single morning or evening or transition with your child due to her total defiance.

❏   You are really trying to be a nicer/better/less screamy parent, but every transition turns you into a bossy parent, despite your best attempts.

❏   You don't see an end in sight; no one's behavior is getting better.

❏   You have more charts, contracts, jars of marbles, stickers, apps, rewards, and punishments than all of the preschools on the East Coast combined, and they are all utter failures.

❏   You have purchased at least two books with titles like *Loving Your Defiant Devil-Child* and *Your Child Doesn't Listen to You Because You Are a Subpar Parent.*

❏   You have googled phrases like "Why doesn't my child listen to me?" and "Why are other people's children so much better than mine?" and "More creative punishments for children who don't listen because everything has stopped working."

Is the above list a be-all and end-all of the potential problems with your child? No! This list is just one tool (of many) that may help you zoom out of the day-to-day struggle and refocus on the larger issues in your relationship. And if the majority of this list speaks to you, don't feel discouraged (probably too late for that). You didn't set out to become a bossy parent! Remember, it all started with a healthy parenting instinct to guide and lead your small baby, but that instinct has morphed into an endless full-blown power struggle with your ever-changing child. Our children have matured and changed, and we haven't. It happens all the time.

But.

Staying in reaction mode, making constant demands, and giving commands is an exhausting way to parent. Period. It creates much unneeded drama, frustration, and anger, and chips away at your relationship with your child. Am I asking you to stop having expectations of your child altogether? No, I have never met a decent parent who doesn't make demands on her child. As parents, it is our obligation to bring structure and routine to our children, and that routine mandates that we are the driver of this family clown car. Your instinct to lead, guide, and expect cooperation is not the problem.

What, then, is the problem with our commands and demands? How are we meant to lead and not be overly bossy at the same time? If we are meant to steer and guide, why does all this steering and demanding and drive-by parenting create so many difficulties and mayhem and fighting?

Why do our children resist our parenting so damn much?

Let's look at an example to further explain how we got into this pickle, and then we will figure out how we can get out of it.

I am the mother to three children. Three girls. And each is so different from the other, it is stunning to think my husband and I made them together. My middle child, Weezy (her name is Louise, but she goes by Weezy because that is who she is), has a unique personality. Born an old soul, her ability to laser-focus on activities she loves is unparalleled. In fact, if I could bottle her focus, I would be a billionaire. It is better than the best Adderall.

When she was around four years old, Weezy became obsessed with Legos and building. Unlike her older sister (seven at the time), who was hopping out of bed, brushing her teeth, and happily getting herself dressed, Weezy would mosey through the house until her eyes would light upon a Lego project. She would sit down, and in a blink, she was utterly lost to me. She would sit in front of the project, half-eaten waffles next to her, and begin her work. She became completely unresponsive to all of my commands and demands. It was a disaster. Was I happy she loved building and did I love her focus? Of course! Dreams of her award-winning architecture filled my mind. It was that the timing of these beautiful attributes was incredibly inconvenient for me. I had three children to get out the door, and her love of Lego building in the morning wasn't working for me.

My mornings became filled with bossiness and drive-by parenting of the worst sort. I would walk from room to room, carrying diapers and shoes, paper towels and cereal, yelling over my shoulder in her general direction (please imagine this in a slightly Philadelphia/Delaware accent . . . not pretty):

"Weezy, stop building and please get your clothes on."

"Weezy, sit down and finish your waffle."

"Weezy, did you hear me?"

"Weezy, where are your sandals?"

"Weezy, did you hear me?"

"WEEZY?!"

By the last "Weezy!" I am ashamed to admit that the drive-by commands were now an all-out missile assault to the top of her head. I would be whisper-yelling, leaning over her, my anger boiling over. I would be issuing threats I would never make good on: "I am going to throw out all of your Legos!" or "That's it; I am leaving for school without you!" or "If you don't get up now, I am canceling your birthday party!" Her big, blue, shocked eyes would fill with tears and she would run and hide. Just typing that fills me with shame. She was (and is) so sensitive that it would take hours, sometimes days, to bring her back into trust and eye contact with me again. But I am telling you this story not to shame myself, but to let you know how ordinary drive-by parenting can be. (Parent coaches: They're just like us.)

I was at the end of my rope. I had three small children, no real help in the morning shuffle, and a child who would not take directions from me. In my heart, I knew she wasn't trying to torture me, but I couldn't see this problem another way. It sure *felt* like she was trying to torture me. Every morning, my goal was to not scream, not boss, and not yell at the top of her head, but you cannot just achieve a negative goal in parenting. Stopping what doesn't work is a necessary first step in changing (see Chapter 4), but if you don't replace the negative behavior with something positive, you will always revert to old ways. Why? Because your brain will go back to what feels comfortable, even if it flies in the face of all sense and reason. Even if you are miserable! So, promising myself I would stop screaming like a lunatic would work for about three days and then, despite my best intentions and desperation, I would revert to commanding, demanding, and eventually hollering at Louise while I dashed from one room to another. Classic drive-by parenting.

I needed a positive goal.

I wrote it down because the more real you make your goal, the more of a chance you give yourself to achieve that goal:

I aspire to peacefully help Louise complete her morning routine.

My Buddhist teacher, Karen Maezen Miller, told me to use the word "aspire" because it means that you try to guide one's hopes or ambitions toward achieving a goal. Before, I had always "wanted" something to happen, and *wanting* seeks to possess something or someone. Wanting something connotes an intrinsic lack, and I would prefer to be the person who guides my hopes rather than tries to fill a lack or a void. Can you feel the energetic difference between the two words, between aspiring and wanting in your parenting life?

I needed to look at what was really happening with Weezy in order to find my aspiration. What were the real problems in my morning? The obvious difficulty was that Louise loved (and was distracted by) her projects, and I could not get her to focus on the tasks at hand. In the moment of my righteous anger, she was the problem and I was the victim of her misbehavior. In my frazzled mind, had I actually begun to believe that my four-year-old was out to get me? Good grief, talk about misguided. I really thought that this child awoke every morning with the intention of making my life hell. Deep down I knew better, but this is what an exhausted and frustrated mind does: It assigns blame to the blameless.

Was my daughter at fault for this dynamic? Was it her fault that I was drive-by parenting all over the place? No. Not even close. In order to improve our mornings, the first thing I had to do was acknowledge this first fact: Weezy was not out to get me. She was not consciously intending to ignore me or shirk her four-year-old duties, nor was her behavior intended to anger me.

My anger was not my child's fault.

Do you know how hard that was for me to accept? For me to accept and own all of my ugly emotions and behavior? Needless to say, it was sobering, but when I decided that my child is actually a child and maybe she was not the sole problem, I immediately felt lighter. I looked at Weezy with new eyes, with compassion. Here was a little girl who loved to play and build, and she was happy. Yes, this was inconvenient, but this was not *misbehavior.* There is nothing "wrong" with her for wanting to play, and furthermore, there was nothing wrong with me for being frustrated. My frustration was also normal. Huh. Acknowledging my daughter's humanity forced me to acknowledge my own imperfections and flaws, as well as forgive myself.

Are you too bossy and explosive with your children? And do you blame your children for your bossiness, explosiveness, and drive-by parenting? Maybe. Maybe you have some major growing up to do, but go ahead and extend some love to yourself. I promise, it won't hurt you. We have all been in a position where we wished we were better, more mature, more loving, and more patient. We have all lacked in emotional maturity, and like dieting, punishing ourselves into change doesn't work. Never has, never will. Simply forgive yourself and move forward.

This big realization, the realization that my daughter was not personally attacking me, did not immediately fix our problems in the morning routine, but by realizing that my child was not personally trying to anger me, I was able to find a more peaceful solution to my drive-by parenting. Without this compassionate and loving stance, without kindness and appreciation of her development and her unique personality, I would have persisted in finding solutions that tore us apart. I would have switched from drive-by parenting to counting to three (Any counters in the house? Raise your hand!) to putting her on a step (Ah, our favorite! The unsuccessful time-outs!) to taking things away to, well, who knows what else? Without generosity of spirit, I would have disconnected from her, not connected with her.

Once you have acknowledged your humanity and that all parents are flawed, and once you see that many of us are drive-by parents, you are ready to learn about one of the most powerful tools I use in my coaching (and the tool that I have already talked about in this book): looking for patterns. Seeing our patterns (in our thoughts, in our family dynamics, and in our parenting behaviors) is a way to clarify what you need to change and why you need to change it. Why do we need to understand our patterns in order to help our parenting lives and stop drive-by parenting? Because without the ability to do this, we are no better than the next mammal! Think about it: Our amazing brains have the ability to think about our own thoughts, and this is an exciting gift! True, it makes us a little neurotic, but it also gives us the power to see clearly; we have the power to change!

When I wrote down (pen and paper) what was happening with Weezy, I found that, to begin with, I was not organized enough in the morning.* I was drive-by parenting because I was running late, I was not prepared for the morning hustle, and I was chronically trying to beat the clock.

Over the years of working with parents, I have seen how time has played a crucial role in the rate of drive-by parenting happening in the family. The more that time (or a lack of time) is an issue in a power struggle with a child, the bossier we become. When we parents feel like we are running late, our brains often go into full-on panic mode, exacerbating our need to control and command everyone and everything in front of us. It can be very hard to override this neural wiring, so rather than fighting our natures tooth and nail, we can plan ahead and sidestep the time crisis rather than trying to endure it.

I repeat: It is easier to plan ahead and sidestep this crisis rather than trying to endure it.

---

* It is important to write by hand. Why? Google "the power of handwriting something rather than typing," and read the studies. Handwriting activates our brains in ways that typing doesn't and we need all the activation we can get. If you prefer to type, then type, but also give handwriting a try.

I had to clean up my organizational act. I am not the tidiest (coughs and looks away) person in the world, but a couple of simple morning changes did the trick. I got my coffee and lunches ready the night before, I set the breakfast table the night before, and I made sure all the little backpacks and shoes were ready to go by the door. I also began to make a list of my appointments as well as keep my to-do list next to my bed. I eventually would use a bullet journal, but this was the first iteration of helping my brain remember what was coming down the pike. Nothing crazy, just small and doable tweaks in my routine that left me feeling less panicked, more in control, and most important, feeling like I had time to pay attention to my children (especially Weezy) in the morning.

And, it is important for me to point this out: I get really pissed off when people suggest doing "everything the night before." I have read countless columns, blogs, and articles detailing how one can get a jump on the day, and never once have I appreciated or received them with anything other than an eye roll. I have sat back, taken a good look at my disgust, and have come to this conclusion: I am disgusted with these suggestions because I know they are true. Whether I get my act together the night before or awaken earlier in the morning, there was no sidestepping the reality that I needed to get more organized. If you have a bunch of kids (or one) and they are little, *this is the deal.* I fought this reality for a bit, but when I finally grew up and faced my life, I could see that this was a crucial part of the parenting gig.

What Else Is Really Happening Here?

What else was coming up when I analyzed the patterns of my drive-by parenting? Hmmm, well, I seemed to be losing Weezy's attention between her getting dressed and her eating breakfast. As I tended to the baby and got the breakfast ready, Weezy was ambling away to search out her Legos. This is where she needed more guidance. I was regularly yelling when the kids were supposed to be eating. I created a plan where I kept the baby on my hip and held firmly onto Weezy's hand after getting her dressed. I essentially chatted with Weezy and led her to the breakfast table in a firm and loving way. I may have asked her to help me with her little sister or I may have asked her to pour cereal, but either way I had to keep her interested and at the table. It was on me to ensure I interrupted the pattern of her meandering away. I had to repeatedly steer her away from the Legos, but when I zoomed out, it was apparent that I was waiting on a four-year-old to do all of the changing in the relationship when it was me that needed to change the conditions.

Was this annoying, all this handholding and guidance? Hell, yes! But it was less annoying than the yelling.

And so, I was left with an important question: When *could* Louise build her Legos? In order to make room for the Legos in the morning, I needed a simple routine of what Louise and I needed to get done, and we both needed to see that reminder every morning: "We are going to play with the Legos when we are finished with our morning duties." We created a little poster board with "the four things that have to happen every morning." Brushing teeth, getting dressed, eating breakfast, putting on shoes. Very simple, very clear instructions for her. When these tasks were complete, I set the alarm and allowed her play with her Legos for as much time as we had left.

To review: 1) I realized that I was hollering at Louise because she was wandering off to build her Legos. 2) I acknowledged that it was not my child's fault that I was so angry and out of control; it was my fault (and I forgave myself). 3) In the patterns, I saw that I was disorganized, and in the morning rush, I had lost Louise to the Legos. 4) I wanted us to stick to a routine, so I needed to make one for both of us (cue the poster board).

See all of those neat and easy solutions? Boom. Done. Everything was just *perfect* after I simply grew up, accepted my daughter, forgave myself, happily zoomed out, clearly and quickly saw my broken patterns, and perfectly applied clear and obvious solutions. I COMPLETELY STOPPED MY DRIVE-BY PARENTING ISSUES. Insert cheerleader kick here.

Uh . . . no.

Because life is messy and humans are imperfect, my plan worked about 73 percent of the time. This means that there was about 27 percent of the time that I was definitely not sticking to my plan. A sick child (or parent), hormones, growth spurts, school problems, work problems, too much rain, too much heat, too much cold, not enough sleep, or just general life suckiness got in the way of my lovely and perfectly crafted solutions. Life happens! My children grew, old problems fell away, and new problems sprouted in their place. And despite my best intentions, I would lose my cool and shout commands and make demands on my children. I still do, to this day.

If you are going to rein in your drive-by parenting, here is a detail you are going to have to accept: The steps you take to solve your problems, the solutions you find, the strategies you employ . . . none of them are transactional. Just because you wake up to your parenting life and make wonderful changes doesn't obligate your child to fall into line, too. It is sobering, but I find it liberating to know that parenting isn't an "If A, then B" setup. It leaves me latitude and freedom to be imperfect, to wake up and keep trying. Parenting without limits, baby!

But you may read my story about Weezy and the Legos and think that there is no way you can make changes like this; all this zooming out and writing down and changing of your own behaviors, day after day. You may believe that you are too angry, too broken, too resentful, and too entrenched in your ways to stop nagging your child. Maybe you feel too tired, too beaten down, and too unsupported. You may wonder why you are the one who's always left holding the bag, doing all of the emotional heavy lifting for the family. I hear you.

I have coached parents who have experienced some of the most harrowing circumstances I have ever heard, and simply asking them to step out of the minutiae was all they could handle. Seeing the patterns (*not* creating and implementing solutions) was their first and only practice for a good long while. Try it; it can utterly change your drive-by parenting habits! Spend one week asking yourself this question: "What is *really* happening here?" Make it an alert in your smartphone, an event in your calendar, and hang sticky notes wherever you spend the most time to remind yourself to have perspective. Seeing your child and yourself clearly is profound, and that clarity *can* change your own parenting behavior. No matter your circumstances, you have the power to change one small aspect of your thinking. You have the power to stop harassing your child. You know that drive-by parenting will (a) never get you what you want in your relationship with your child; (b) bring more fights and resistance than you can ever imagine; and (c) not resolve itself with time, so any move in a different direction is worth it.

REFLECT AND WRITE

1. Do you hate the sound of your own voice because all you do is boss your child around? Do you actually use a quiet, passive-aggressive, whiny voice that may actually be worse than yelling (death by a thousand cuts)?

2. Are your requests ignored every single time? BTW, it is totally normal for your children to sometimes ignore you because, well, they are kids.

3. Are your demands age-appropriate? Telling a four-year-old to "clean his room" is an example of an inappropriate command. I have a list of resources in the back to figure out what is appropriate, but in this instance, Google is your friend.

4. Do you make up stuff for your children to do as you walk around the house? Like "Why are these clothes out? Put them away. And these Pokémon cards shouldn't be here. Take them to your room . . . and while you are up there, make your bed and then come down here and get your cereal bowl off the table . . ." You are just shooting from the hip, commanding and demanding without sense or reason. This is super stressful. Can you find a time to hand out a *short* to-do list?

5. Have your kids started to fight you on even the most basic of tasks? Does it feel like your children scream "no" even before you end your sentence? Is the screaming and defiance getting worse? Does this happen at certain times in the day or during certain transitions?

6. Have your children started ghosting you completely? Like, you make one demand and poof! The children are gone? Are you finding yourself screaming down hallways and upstairs things like, "I know you heard

me! Get down here. Sam, I know you can hear me!
Sam? Sam!"

7.   Do you feel resentful, depressed, and worried that you are
       raising brats?

8.   Can you take responsibility for your own behavior? Can
       you find compassion for your child? Can you see that your
       child is not trying to ruin your life? If your answer is "No,
       Meghan. This is 100 percent my child's fault," then you
       have to stay right here and figure this out. And trust me, I
       get it. Maybe you are parenting a child with executive
       functioning issues, and said child cannot get from A to B
       without meandering for two hours. Maybe you are par-
       enting a sensitive child for whom every command feels
       like an assault, even when you are using the gentlest and
       kindest of tones. Maybe you are grieving a loss and are
       quick to anger and frustration. Maybe your marriage is
       feeling fraught and your parenting life feels unsupported
       and adrift. I hear you. Life is hard and messy. And still,
       the cold reality is that our children are still not responsible
       for our behavior. Go ahead and get support for your
       anger, depression, anxiety, grief, and isolation. Find spe-
       cialists for your child. Take all the time you need. If un-
       derstanding your drive-by parenting leads you to what
       seems like the very bottom, good! That's the best place to
       begin. Why? Because it is real. You can actually do some-
       thing from there; you can push up from the bottom. I am
       not being cavalier here, either. Finding specialists and
       therapists and helpers is no small task. It can take days,

weeks, and months to find your team, and if this is all you do after you read this chapter? Winner-winner, chicken dinner.

9. Does your routine need a refresh? Did it use to work and now your family has seemed to outgrow it? Did your routine ever work to begin with? What elements of your routine feel out of control?

CHAPTER 8

Your Child Doesn't Give a Shit About Your Organic Salmon

If you haven't yet, at some point you will feel guilty about the chicken nuggets, mac 'n' cheese, and frozen peas that you keep feeding your children and you will make a "new plan" for dinner. If you haven't reached this point in your parenting life, it is because:

1. Your children are little and you are still feeding them a mix of baby food and whatever you are eating.

2. You are whipping up huge batches of homemade food and would rather die than allow your child to eat a nugget.

3. You are not the one feeding your children. Nanny, spouse, daycare, Grandma, someone else is responsible for this onerous task, so count yourself among the lucky.

If you are one of the three people above, you should still read this chapter as a cautionary tale: a tale of what happens when we make plans in our heads that have little chance of actually working.

Maybe, by way of example, you have realized that you have gone overboard on the chicken nuggets or microwaved food and you can hear your children's taste buds dying every night. You have decided on a new plan for your child to eat something healthy and wholesome. Your children will eat fish—salmon, specifically. This plan may spring from your own childhood memories of complete dinners served at six o'clock sharp; this plan may come from seeing the Instagram posts of delicious meals served to smiling children; this plan may come from remembering that you only ate dinners dumped out of a can and you resent the hell out of that; this plan may come from your cousin's fortieth post on Facebook, explaining how delicious and easy her new cookbook is; this plan may come from an "easy and delicious" food delivery service (see Blue Apron); or this plan may simply come from the embarrassment that your children can no longer eat in a restaurant or another home unless nuggets are served.

Whatever it is, you will decide to get those fatty omegas and vitamins into your children, come hell or high water. You will google "child-friendly salmon recipes" and you will go to your local Whole Foods and spend $700,000 on salmon (fresh, never frozen, as well as sustainably farmed) plus organic dill and crème fraîche. You will make a side of brown rice and a green salad with grape tomatoes, cucumbers, and homemade vinaigrette. You will not serve organic juice or Capri Sun; the children will drink water or organic milk (from a nearby farm). *And they will love it.*

True, you forgot to have the fishmonger take the skin off the salmon and you will hack away at the $5,000 fish as the children fight in the background. True, you will forget that the brown rice takes almost an hour to make and yours will take a full fifty minutes, completely screwing up your time line for dinner. True, you forgot that cutting a million grape tomatoes is like trying to hold on to a greased pig (those fuckers really slide and skitter everywhere), and you will spend at least five minutes picking them up off the floor. But no matter.

DEEEENAR. IZZZ. AH-SAAAARVED.

Now, the children will have already mentioned once, twice, or three hundred times that they are "definitely not eating this disgusting dinner," as you struggled to prepare it. As the fish is served, one child may begin to whine as the other child goes digging into the freezer for the nuggets. They may refuse to sit down and then once they do, the children will poke and prod and push around the fish like it is roadkill. The rice, while fluffy and delicious, is not covered in cheese sauce or butter (and therefore not getting touched), and the children refuse to even look at the salad. Your partner (who didn't know that salmon was going to be served) will look both amused and annoyed, because he or she knows exactly how this is going to go down. This dinner is going to be a disaster. Like a choose-your-own-ending book, you can imagine where this dinner may go next, and it isn't the ending where the children eat and thank their smiling parents. Threats, punishments, crying, stomp-offs, refusals to "take a taste," stubbornness, and hurt feelings will abound and it all ends with bowls of cereal and cold salmon. What went wrong?

Well, not to beat a metaphor to death, but the salmon dinner represents our parenting expectations and how we are constantly setting ourselves up for hurt feelings and seething anger.

Oh, don't get me wrong. I am not blaming us parents for wanting our children to happily eat the organic salmon. We are not robots. We have hopes and dreams and longings like every other human out there, and when we make an effort—when we care so *very, very* much—the denial to eat our food feels like a smack in the face. The ingratitude, the outright defiance, and the disrespect is jarring and it can cut us to the quick.

Though I am not sure it can be substantiated by science, I think there is something built into our parenting DNA where we expect our children to accept our offerings. We anticipate that we can fulfill our children's needs, and when we cannot, it is surprising and very upsetting. Beyond our hurt feelings, we also begin to create stories of how our children are ungrateful brats. In front of our eyes, our children morph into little Bernie Madoffs, abusing others and taking for granted everything good in the world. The panic of raising a spoiled brat makes most of us so crazy that we double down into the most insane power struggles that have ever been created. (Unless you are a spoiled brat yourself, or you are so scared of conflict with your child that you scurry away at their first outburst . . . If the latter is you, don't worry; there are some chapters just for you in this book.)

You are completely losing your mind over your potentially spoiled child, and it all hinges on them eating this salmon.

And I get it.

I have gone out of my way, hundreds of times, only to have my children scoff at me, blow off my offerings, and outright disrespect my efforts. I have exploded, I have sent children to rooms without food, and I have made threats that I could only make good on if I were prepared to cancel birthday parties and expensive family trips.

In essence, the salmon represents so many efforts in our parenting lives.

I once coached a parent who was desperate to connect with her shy eight-year-old son. She just wanted to laugh with him, have a good time. She took him to an amusement park (which is a heavy lift for even the most extroverted of humans), and he did not appreciate this gesture. He sulked, he didn't care about the rides, he didn't want popcorn, it was too hot, the lines were too long, and he wanted to go home.

The mother was apoplectic. "I did all the things!" she cried on the phone. She cared, she went out of her way, she created and executed a plan, and as Dorinda Medley says on *The Real Housewives of New York City*, "I made it nice." The mom was understandably crushed, but this experience with her son, this expectation dressed up as an amusement park? This was her greatest lesson. How so?

She learned that her desires and expectations, and even good deeds, are not transactional agreements with her child.

SAY WUT.

That's right! Your children don't owe you joy. They don't even owe you gratitude.

Your children don't owe you joy.

"How can this be?" you may be screaming at this book. And if you were born before the 1990s, you may also be telling yourself a story about, "Well, if I didn't respect my parents, they would have whooped my ass," or "This is what's wrong with parenting today! Our kids aren't expected to respect us!"

I am going to propose that what you are calling respect may actually be fear, and *never* in the history of humanity has true respect been born out of pure fear, but that's an aside. The truth is that we limit our parenting lives a great deal when we parent our children so that they will be *happy*. We are limited when we confuse our gestures of love with promises of gratitude and good behavior from our children. It doesn't work that way; at least, not right away. Where did we go sideways in our parenting with our salmon and our amusement parks and our expectations?

Where did we go wrong with our hopes of gratitude and respect?

Leggo My Ego

We didn't really go wrong; it's just that we are placing all our hopes on the shoulders of a child. Read that again: We, the adults, are expecting a child to make us happy, fulfilled, and righteous. Our egos are dragging us around by the nose, and if we want to have a shot at actually enjoying the children in front of us, we gotta see this truth for what it is.

Let's walk it out: Once upon a time, I made pseudo-normal dinners for my children (a protein, a veggie, a healthy carb) until they screamed, "No!" Exhausted and annoyed and unable to handle the no's due to my own crappy self-care and life in general, I started making nuggets and never stopped (like all good drugs, the nuggets were cheap, easy to get, and soooo good). And this was great. Everyone ate and everyone stopped screaming at me. Peace ruled the land.

And then, because I am a conscious human and my intuition began to gently knock, I realized that my children were now made of 90 percent Goldfish crackers and organic nuggets, and I needed to do better. In my mind, I made some big decisions about my children and their health, and presto! This was going to work because *I decided it and I wanted it to work.*

When I announced my desire for everyone to start eating healthy fish, what I was really saying to my children (and spouse) was, "I am now doing the opposite of everything I have ever done, kiddos. First, I expect you to give me zero pushback for this drastic change in our eating and, second, I want you to be grateful."

Think about this: I had served my children what they had begged for, but now I was pissed at them for not handling my abrupt changes with gratitude and smiles.

This is as illogical as you can get, no?

The amusement park mom? She's a good and loving parent who was (and is) trying, but you don't undo months and months of disconnection with a trip to Busch Gardens. A plus B does not equal C when it comes to human connection, especially children.

Let's say your partner or friend lets you down, every day; it chips away at your soul. And then this person announces, "Everything is different! I am changing! And here is a little gift, too." Has the proclamation or trinket changed a thing? Maybe you are hopeful, but no, it has changed nothing about your relationship. All you need to do is watch *The Bachelor* to see how words and gifts do not translate into action or changed feelings. No, we need to see this partner or friend slowly and steadily prove *that* they are different now. And when you don't trust them right away, this person shouldn't berate you into trust. Rather, they get it: They are patient; they understand. They know that trust is earned, not bought or traded.

But we parents? We are working with children. Their inherent immaturity stands like a roadblock in everything we try to do and this is frustrating. If my children hadn't started screaming in the first place, I never would have to have given them all the nuggets to begin with . . . see? Do you see how I just placed the blame of my actions on my young children?

I am not asking you to give up nor am I asking you to let go of any changes you dream of making. No! It is parental obligation to wake up and make changes when you see fit! I am asking you to bring some gentleness, some ease, some space, and some grace to your expectations of how you think this will all go. Above all, I am asking you to see that what you call "relationship building" may actually be transactional and conditional love (ouch). For example, a couple of years ago, I had a big decision to make with my eldest daughter. My expec-tation, stories, reality, all of it was mixed together and I needed help. When I called my teacher, Maezen, she reminded me: "None of the decisions you make are transactional! You cannot guarantee an expe-rience nor can you expect your daughter to become a different person based on any particular decision." Yikes. Oh sure, I needed to hold on to some expectations; I lived in the world of natural consequences just like you, but I understood exactly what Maezen was saying to me: My parenting responsibility was to make the clearest and best decision for my daughter without expectation of her gratitude to make me feel good about it.

Our parenting expectations—like the salmon dinners and amuse-ment parks, saying "I love you" to hear it said back, the "I am being nice to you so that you can be nice to me"—and then all of the blowouts that follow these expectations? Every single parent battles this reality. Every parent battles balancing expectations with discipline and what is real. Every parent sits on their bed, their head in their hands, and wonders where the hell they went wrong.

"When did I believe that family life would be easy?"

"How did I think this dinner was really going to go?"

"When did I believe that my child's school choice would save my family?"

"What did I think the birth of my child was going to be like?"

"What type of learner did I think my child would be?"

"How did I think my marriage would adapt to the addition of children?"

"Did I think my child would stay warm and cuddly forever?"

"When did I believe my child would not make some big mistakes?"

If you have not yet sat on the edge of your bed, wrestling with your own ego and fear, your day is coming. And don't worry, you can handle it.

My big revelation came with that salmon dinner. Similar to leaving the full grocery cart in the aisle and shoving a shirt over my daughter's head, I clearly saw the prison I had built for myself. I wasn't happy with the vision, but the clarity felt like relief.

I began with a family meeting. "Guys, I love nuggets. And we are always going to eat nuggets. *And* we are going to start throwing some other foods in so that you can grow and have a more sophisticated palate." (Use big words; it keeps them on their toes!) "We are going to take bites and try things. Why do you think this is important?"

I gathered their thoughts, we made deals about what would get served (some pasta and fruit), and like water dripping on a stone, we made some small progress on this food debacle. Don't think your children are old enough for family meetings? Wrong. Think your children are too old for you to begin family meetings? Wrong again. Children of all ages love to have their voices heard, to feel respected, and to feel like they matter. As long as you keep adjusting your expectations to their developmental and emotional stages, you will make a dent in the debacle. Slow and steady. The family meeting may yield compromises such as (these were our meeting notes):

- Having meals that end in cereal

- Having meals where part of what's on the plate sits untouched

- Being allowed to nag your child a maximum of three times

All valid!

But slowly and surely, your children will begin to eat the food you serve them. And here's the secret sauce to fixing all of these false expectations: connection. When I dropped the food as the main issue and began to focus on meals being a time of laughter, asking thoughtful questions, making eye contact, smiling, and connecting? Everything changed. There are so many studies that show that children who share meals with their parents do fewer drugs and have fewer early pregnancies, and this sure as hell ain't about the food. It's about the fulfillment of connection; the deep human need to feel seen and heard! This is so true that, when I coach parents who are in crisis and everything is going wrong, do you think I give a damn about nuggets? No. I will say, "Sit with the children and eat the nuggets. Laugh and look them in the eyes and make it short and sweet." Good and nutritious foods matter, but connection matters more.

Nutritious foods matter, but connection matters more.

The amusement park mom? She didn't need all the bells and whistles (literally). She needed to get into her son's world and just enjoy him, bit by bit. Like drops of water in an empty cup, she needed to fill him up slowly. And it was still okay she did the whole amusement park outing, because she learned that her son didn't need the fanciness and the big gift. Instead, they sat on the couch and he taught her how Minecraft works.

By not rushing to fulfill our parental expectations, as well as not rushing our children to appreciate us, we cultivate the very gratitude that we long to see in our children.

Take steps toward seeing what you are doing when you burden your children with your expectations! See your habits, watch your expectations dressed up as hope, assess if what you are doing is building a relationship with your child or tearing it down, and understand that parenting is a long-game effort.

And in case the salmon dinner and amusement park feel like "big gestures," please know it is the smallest of assumptions and the most casual neediness that chips away at our parent-child relationships. Examples?

> *"Aren't you happy with the sneakers I got you? They weren't cheap."*

> *"Isn't it nice I stayed for your game? I worked longer last night so I could be here."*

> *"I don't embarrass you in front of your friends, isn't that nice?"*

> *"I made those cupcakes from scratch. Aren't they better than store-bought?"*

"I found all your socks under your bed and washed them . . .
What do you think of that?"

And when our children are not behaving gratefully enough (for us), we will demand and guilt the gratitude out of them.

"Have you seen the kids in [insert the country devastated by a recent
natural disaster]? They have nothing. They would eat this
broccoli, happily."

"You should have seen my clothes when I was your age. I never got
this kind of stuff . . . If you saw what I had, you would be singing
another tune . . ."

"Do you think I want to drive over hill and dale for your practices
while you whine? You should see how much I spend on gas . . ."

"How about a thank-you *for doing everything for everyone in*
this family, every single day?"

These little statements can fly out of our mouths so casually; we may not even be aware we do it. Some of us chalk it up to being Catholic or Jewish or Italian or Greek or Baptist or whatever religion or culture you identify with, but the truth? Everyone is susceptible to this, and guilting our kids into gratitude sucks. It doesn't make them grateful and it doesn't make them better people. It makes them resent us as well as increases unappreciative behavior. Am I saying there isn't a time to check our kids and their privilege? No. There is absolutely a time and a place, but if you have created the circumstances (e.g., driving them everywhere), you have to own that. Firstly, you did that and secondly, the children are now used to the privilege. You have created your own monster, and guilt won't help quell it.

So, what are you supposed to do about gratitude and expectations, other than stay silent and pray that your child won't become a holy terror? Here are some ideas:

- **Make a plan with your family.** Like the food family meeting, decide how to fold the children into the changes you want to make. Unless the discouragement runs really deep, children are often happy to help create another (healthier) dynamic in the family.

- **Practice keeping your piehole shut.** When I drive my daughter to school when she could have walked, I desperately want her to thank me and hug me and love me; instead, I just listen to the radio. I just . . . don't say a word. I chose to drive her; all I need to do is apply the gas, push on the brake, and kiss her goodbye.

- **In the words of Iyanla Vanzant, "Call a thing a thing."** Say, "I know you are tired and hungry and this car ride is boring. I would also like for you to stop complaining. I am losing my patience, and I want silence. Now." Or, "I know you are sick of soup and salad, but this is what is being served. Your whining is beginning to get to me. Stop it." Parents, if you want to say something, *then say it*. You don't have to attack the children or name-call or be passive-aggressive. Just tell them, "Stop it!" They may sit and sulk or hate you or wish you were dead, but at least you aren't listening to their voice anymore. And trust me, every person in your child's future will thank you for calling a thing a thing.

- **Take a peek at how you may be twisting yourself into an emotional and physical pretzel, and realize this:** *No one asked you to do that.* If you have built a whole parenting narrative around your perceived slights and expectations, then it's all on you. Don't panic: It's a *good* thing that it's all on you. It means you aren't responsible for changing anyone else. What can you let go of? Where are you not needed? What can you excuse yourself from? If you aren't sure, ask your spouse and friends . . . If they are honest people, they will tell you.

I know that the idea of not commanding and demanding respect, love, and obedience from our children (as well as receiving it) is somewhat controversial. I know that there is a natural hierarchy of adults and children in which parents *must* lead and children *should* follow. I am not disputing that dynamic; in fact, being a weak leader is a family disaster. I am just floating the idea that expecting appreciation and change doesn't make it so (especially when it comes to our children), and we can save ourselves a lot of grief if we accept this fact. We can open up more space for positive and deeper interactions.

REFLECT AND WRITE

1.   Think of an example, in your parenting life, when you tried to do something positive and it was met with harsh

resistance. What were the stories guiding that? Were they true? (Sometimes they are!)

2. Did you grow up with conditional love? Meaning you had to constantly earn your parents' affection?

3. Do you believe that the gratitude that you seek will come eventually? Can you accept the idea of never seeing it?

4. Is there a change you want to make now? Who else can support you in this change? Can the kids be brought in? How can you spread the work and effort around?

Seven Ways to Make Dinner with Kids Easier: Pick One
(Any One)

Although I wrote a chapter about expectations disguised as my salmon dinner, I do acknowledge that dinner is a wretched time for many families. The following dinner tips are meant for you to use however *you* want. Use one. Use all. Whatever works best for *your* family.

1. **Recognize that kids don't typically have much of an appetite for dinner.** They have front-loaded their calories (which is good) and are not interested in your meatloaf at 6:00 p.m. It isn't personal.

2. **Have the children help you meal plan.** They can pick a protein, a carbohydrate, and a veggie, and create a dinner one night a week or more. The more invested the child is in

the food, the more likely they are to eat it. I find that tacos almost always work, BTW.

3. **Have the children help you make the dinner.** Tearing and washing lettuce, stirring, mashing . . . these are all tasks children can perform, from even very young ages. The sense of pride a child has when they have contributed can work meal-time miracles. Yes, you have to be emotionally and physically ready for this, parents. You have to stay patient and loving, because your children are learning; they are not sous-chefs.

4. **Keep the focus on the family and chatting at mealtime, not the food.** Ask each other interesting questions, such as: If you were a color, which one would you be? If you had to live in one room in the house, which one would you choose? Which superpower would you want and why? Questions like this spur interesting conversations; a question like "What did you do in school today?" is *not* an interesting question. The difference between a family dinner being miserable or somewhat pleasant comes down to this very strategy; to the degree that I can stay lighthearted and conversational, our dinners are pleasant.

5. **Do not count bites.** "Three more bites of peas" is food policing, and unless your child has a medical issue, this is not a way to spend a meal (and even then, counting bites *bites*). Bite-counting encourages food paranoia, and yes, it can even encourage disordered eating later (sorry to be such a downer). Instead, notice when your child tries something: "I see you tried your peas! Delicious, right?" Encouraging

the behavior you want to see will get you further, but play it cool. Too much cheerleading will lead the child to do the opposite, too. Oy.

6.   **Do not offer dessert as a reward for finishing dinner.** This makes children sweet-obsessed and turns you into the food police again. Some better ideas? Dessert is offered Friday and Saturday nights, and the children can eat it whenever they want during the meal. Or offer dessert every night, no matter the dinner eaten (yup, I just wrote that). The point is: Stop making dessert conditional on eating dinner all of the time. Again, it can lead to disordered eating, hiding, sneaking, and bingeing.

7.   **Most important, remember that dinner is a time for the whole family to come together, share, laugh, and simply enjoy each other.** Try not to get mired down in the food choices and number of bites. Stay positive, stay smiling, and try to truly enjoy their company. You will be surprised how quickly the children will follow your lead.

CHAPTER 9

Is It Your Child Who Is Addicted to Technology and Turning into a Zombie in Front of Your Eyes . . . or Is It You?

Every single parent I speak to is rightly worried about technology and its stranglehold on children. We have watched technology change every aspect of our lives, and many of us lament that the experiences of our footloose and fancy-free childhoods are gone for good. How can children experience the beauty of nature, the exhilaration of real adventure, as well as the fun and heartbreak of friendships when they are in front of a screen upward of eight hours a day? (Meanwhile, many of us were latchkey kids who were not frolicking or adventuring, and many of us could have used a ton more active parenting in our lives, but details, details . . .)

Sure, we are in the midst of a "crisis." We in America love an epidemic, and we've made a nice big one for ourselves. As I type this, rehabilitation services are popping up everywhere for children and adolescents who are addicted to technology, gaming in particular. And the data concerning the correlation between depression and anxiety in tween and teen girls (and boys) and their social media life gives every parent chills. We are awash in messages about porn, pedophiles, and pathology. There is bullying, body images, and boredom. Suicide is up. Human connection is down. It is a disaster . . . right?

But I am not a big believer in going full-tilt Chicken Little on this issue, so let's work with this epidemic with a little more aplomb and a little less panic, shall we?

Here's the deal: I am a parent coach, not a child coach, so the first thing I will always want to assess is *your* tech use. Why? Because you cannot pay attention to your children's tech lives and needs if you are lost in your own smartphone and laptop.

And it matters not how busy you are or what kind of job you have; I would bet the farm that you don't need to look at your phone as much as you do. If you are on call to transplant a heart, day in and day out? Fine. If you are waiting for your sister to have a baby? Fine. If you are out and there is a new babysitter in the house, and you want to text here and there? Fine. But, really, what are your other excuses? Getting texts from our friends and checking work emails simply doesn't justify the fact that the phones are glued to us 24/7. Watching the market doesn't count as "necessary" just because you are a bigwig trader. Getting an amazing score on *Candy Crush* is definitely an awesome feeling, but it's also an awful time waster and extraordinarily unnecessary. And staying available for every work notification is not only unnecessary, it's unhealthy.

"But, Meghan . . . my job!" Please. Chances are good that, if you know me at all, you know I am going to call a big ol' BS on that. Not because I don't care about your job or your family's welfare, but because we both know that we have only two real choices here: You are either tethered to our consumerist, constantly dialed-in culture or you are trying to find a way to live in harmony with tech (which means being able to step away from it).

And if you think I have never had an issue with technology and I am sitting here holier than thou, don't worry: I have had *many issues with tech*; it has definitely interrupted my mental health and parenting. For a good long while, all information coming into my smartphone felt immediate and necessary. I (used to) text and scroll when I walked the dog, when I poured my coffee, and when I got out of the shower (hair still dripping). I would return emails before I got out of bed in the morning and before I shut my eyes at night. I was (still sometimes am) addicted to a game called *Wooden Blocks* (like *Tetris*). There have been times where I spiraled into depression and anxiety, assisted and fed by the constant scrolling. Every single post I read or picture I took in or tweet I read fed my insecurity, fear, worry, or jealousy. Every single human was parenting better, wife-ing better, business-owning better, or just generally living better. My brain kept a steady drumbeat: "The earth is dying, the government is failing, humans are suffering, and I suck."

All of this is to say, I was (and still am) susceptible to email and social media abuse.

Most of us are chronically told (and now know) that technology steals time and happiness from us, but did you know that how we use technology can either contribute directly to our *parenting* happiness or misery? How? Well, let's say both of your parents were a bit anxious; this genetic fact raises your chances of being anxious. So, you are born with this genetic anxious predisposition *and* then, let's say, your parents have a messy and ugly divorce when you are four years old (main attachments coming in and out of your life; anger and confusion and unpredictability may have been frequent), and that increased your anxiety, frustration, and distractibility. Now you are an adult and you have coped well enough, but you may also have a full-blown undiagnosed anxiety disorder (and possibly depression). Your brain is patterned and practiced to find problems and, this is very important, to *think* it sees problems, even when everything is hunky-dory. Now, we hand you a 24/7 problem generator called a smartphone. Your brain, already prone to panic and fear, is now constantly activated by this phone. Bing! Bing! Bing! Like a Pavlovian dog, you cannot find rest; and your ability to sort out true and immediate problems in your life (your kids won't stop kicking each other in the head) from quite serious but non-immediate problems (sea levels rising) is greatly diminished. And for the anxious brain, you will either overreact or underreact to your children, leading to parenting mayhem.

And please don't think that you need to have depression or anxiety to feel panicked by our 24/7 plugged-in lifestyle. From kidnapped children on the other coast to dictators ruining countries to the cost of gas going up to a friend's friend's aunt contracting a rare fungus in her foot, all of our brains are taking in everything going wrong, and that is simply too much for even the most healthy psyches to handle. This panic happens to adults everywhere, every day, all over the world, causing us to become increasingly checked out to our actual reality.

When a parent is mentally checked out, overwhelmed, distracted, or spinning like a top, it is the child who takes in the bulk of that energy (or lack thereof). They feel your mood, they see your furrowed brow, and they are still trying to connect with you, despite your distraction. And unlike your spouse or partner, children cannot say to themselves, "This isn't about you, Isabelle. This is Mom's problem." No, the children unconsciously assume that your anger, distraction, and apathy is about them (because remember, children are sorta little narcissists by nature). I am not saying any of this to guilt you; I am saying this because it is true, and acknowledging the truth is important if we are going to get a grip on our tech use and actually *change.*

Am I suggesting that every parent abuses tech and is checked out of reality? No! Maybe you were born with a brain that handles stress with more equanimity than the average Joe. Maybe your early life was shaped by strong attachments who didn't physically or emotionally hurt you. Maybe your temperament is easy and your mood is stable. (My husband is like this and it drives me absolutely bat-shit crazy. Ironic, right?) Maybe your childhood was kind of jacked up, but through therapy and serious mindfulness, you are now Steady Eddie. For you, technology is something that *enhances* your life. You are made happier by your connections to others through gaming, texting, emails, or social media. Your brain actually seeks out and enjoys seeing what others are doing, and (this is very important) your brain doesn't get stuck on all the bad news. You don't scroll and scroll and scroll, wasting hours of your life. You have a healthy relationship with technology, and your children *also* take this energy in! They witness a parent who doesn't have a distraught face, a parent who doesn't look overwhelmed, a parent who likes to share positive stories or who shares the sad stories with empathy. Point is? Our children see it all and take it all in. Our tech lives affect every aspect of our parenting.

Our tech lives affect every aspect of our parenting.

And so, when I coach parents, I want to know this: Are you anxious/depressed/ADD/ADHD/sensitive and how many hours of tech do you take in on a daily basis? (Whatever amount you tell me, I mentally double or triple it.) As a parent coach, I know that the amount of hours we parents spend on our phones, tablets, and computers is a strong indication of where our eyes are and wherever *we* are looking is getting our full attention.

I repeat: *Wherever you are physically looking is getting your full attention.*

I See You

For a long time, I believed that I needed to possess a certain skill set when it came to connecting with my children. I believed I needed to be artsy and constantly engaged in something artsy to ensure my child was learning valuable lessons. I believed I needed to be always reading or playing or somehow furthering my child's understanding of the world. Every one of my parenting actions was driven by a "purpose," and that purpose assumed that I had something in me that my child lacked. I needed to constantly give something to her.

Think about that a moment: I believed my child was a poor little dry sponge and I had to be the constant (spring) water that filled her up. What a burden I placed on myself! But I quickly came to learn that this was not true, and what I needed to offer my children was far simpler and yet quite a bit more challenging.

I simply needed to *see* my children. Fully. When I could be fully present, without agenda and expectations and neediness, my children were happy. And, while I wish this were not the case, *technology steals our ability to be present.* It steals our eyes, our smiles, and our attention. As Dan Siegel (author and neuroscientist) says, "Every human wants to feel felt," and for children, feeling felt is critical for them to feel safe and to grow and mature. When we are half-listening, constantly glancing at a phone, glimpsing at texts, casually scrolling, and checking our email, we are simply not there. We are actually giving some of the worst attention we can possibly give our children: distracted attention. Distracted attention is so detrimental because it keeps our children in a low-grade panic. *Is she listening now? Did Dad hear me this time? Does*

Mom know what I am trying to ask her? When we dip in and out of being fully present, our children literally don't know what to expect, and so will begin a whole host of misbehaviors. From whining to violence, children will (unconsciously) do what is necessary to get and keep our attention, *to keep our eyes.* And since sometimes you are looking at your children and sometimes you are looking at your phone, your child doesn't know what to do. Their brains are in a panic, so they will whine even when you are looking straight at them. I have spoken to parent after parent who cries, "Meghan, I literally sit there for an hour and listen to my child, but they cannot seem to just calm down and trust that I am doing this!" To which I say, "Exactly!" Our children become conditioned to not trusting that we will simply listen to them! They are conditioned to whining for our attention, even after we put down the phone. It is all so frustrating.

But listen, I don't want you to sit and stare at your child all day. Not only is that ridiculous, it would actually be unhelpful to your child. Children don't need or want *constant* interaction with you, and they definitely don't want you staring at them *all day.* What I am suggesting is that when you are going to be present, be fully present. *Fully* give them your eyes. Don't pick up your device. And then, when you need to check a text, email, or scroll, say aloud, "Pardon me, I need to check my phone."

If this sounds like Manners 101, that's because it is. Simply saying aloud, "I am checking my phone," does a couple of things. It brings your attention back to what you are doing, and it also says to the child, "I am paying attention to you, but now I am going to pay attention to this." You are matching your words to your actions. It may sound silly, but think about what is happening: Our child is telling us something in detail, and we are nodding and listening, but then slowly, slowly, we begin to pick up our devices and scroll . . . and so what is happening with our body language? We are making noises like, "Mmmmmm hmmmm, wow, uh-huh, cool . . . neat . . . huh." We may even be nodding! But our eyes are gone, we are not really listening, and our child knows it.

Simply and politely interrupting our child's story and saying, "Honey, pardon me. I need to answer this email, please give me a moment," is matching our attention and eyes to our actual activity. The likelihood of you doing this (interrupting yourself to look at your phone or computer) may feel far-fetched, but it is a worthy endeavor nonetheless. Imagine if, even three times day, you stopped and said, "Pardon me." Imagine how that could change what you are paying attention to and how your child would feel.

Additionally, by interrupting yourself, forcing yourself to use manners, and making eye contact with your children, you will also role-model what it looks like to have good tech manners. Not having your phone out at meals or during serious discussions or at bedtime is a given (right? Right), but showing your children that it is unacceptable and rude to glance at your device while they speak is a huge lesson in tech etiquette.

Now, if you are like me, you may shudder at endlessly listening to all of your children's stories. You may sigh at not being able to do what you want, when you want. Your ego may be screaming, "But I am sooooo important. And I want to look at my phone when I want to!" I get it. I, too, felt (and feel) frustrated at the idea of using my tech responsibly. I just want to sit and scroll the feed of my FB page dedicated to the Real Housewives of Bravo until my eyes bleed. I can hear my whining now: "I do everything for these children; why do I have to keep listening to them? Attending to them?"

When I feel like this, when I hear this tiny, whiny voice, I know that I need a break. Not the kind of break that tech can provide (well, maybe some Netflix and a little bit of scrolling is okay). What I am saying is that you need a break from the role of "parent." Your tank is going on empty and you need to refill it with real and substantial nourishment. So much of my own desire to disappear into my phone and check out of my life is not because I love what I am reading on my phone or because I am learning something. No, what I really want is to check out because there are too many demands on my time, as well as too much day-to-day emotional heavy lifting. Too many to-do lists (made by me), too many forms (thanks, school), too many back-to-back clients (I love them, but come on, Meghan, watch your calendar), too many trips to the store (due to my hatred of lists), too many commitments (again, check the calendar before you RSVP, Meghan), and too many activities for the family (but I thought they would enrich the kids, d'oh!).

For you, the escape into tech could be your sign of a deep ennui, a deep boredom with your life. You may not be creatively or intellectually challenged, and when your brain uncomfortably nudges you with this boredom, scrolling is a much safer option than deciding that you need to change your life in some small (or big) way. Or maybe you work three jobs, there is financial stress, your spouse just got laid off, and scrolling offers you a respite from the fear you are facing. Or maybe your marriage is shaky and scrolling Instagram offers you some happiness. (Who doesn't love kittens?) Maybe your child just got diagnosed with a disability, and while it is a relief to have a word to put to your child, watching YouTube offers you a break from the endless research in front of you. There are a million reasons we zone out with tech, most of them valid. But endlessly scrolling or busying yourself with glowing screens will never satiate the deeper need we humans have to connect to ourselves and others.

Any step toward moving your eyes from the screen to your children (or nature or a real book) is a worthwhile step. For instance, I have had clients put down their phones at 7:45 p.m. (during the bedtime process) because they just weren't present with their children at this time. Powering off their phones didn't translate to miraculous behavior in the children, but it did translate into more patience and compassion from the parents.

If you feel that your screen time is an issue for you in your parenting life, consider the causes and how you can make changes.

REFLECT AND WRITE

1. Do you think chronic scrolling and email checking is created out of sheer habit (our brains love tech, we don't need an excuse!) or do you think you are avoiding something else in your life (hard work, relationship issues, big decisions, health stress, etc.)? Or both?

2. What is your tech or screen abuse go-to? Scrolling? YouTube? Netflix?

3. Which hours of the day is the tech abuse hurting you *the most*? Bedtime, the morning hustle, lunch breaks, after-school hours? Zeroing in on when your tech use is problematic is important.

4. Find two potential times a day for your screen. This isn't for work; this is purely for fun. What are two realistic times that you could zone out? Carpool line, soccer practice, naptime, over coffee, during lunch? We only need two times a day . . . How long you want those times to be is up to you.

5.   When are your *zero screens* times? I know many parents who have to put down the screen beginning at seven o'clock. Powering on your phone after you leave the house in the morning may be your goal. Staying away from screens when your child is doing homework may be a need for you. Choose your times.

6.   Announce to your family that this is your new habit. Announce three facts: You have your zone-out times, you have your no-screen times, and there will be times when you must use your phone and you will do your best to be polite. Thank your family for their patience as you make these changes (and these changes will take the rest of your life).

7.   Take note of the good that happens when you stop looking at screens. Books read, conversations had, faces seen, skies watched—you get it, right?

How Do You Know If **Both** You and Your Child Have Screen Problems?

In the previous chapter, we discussed the importance of dissecting your own tech lifestyle and how your usage trickles down to your parenting. In this chapter, let's assess how the whole family is using tech, and if the usage has become problematic.

You may have a chronic tech issue if your child is abusing or addicted to *Fortnite* (or whatever the game du jour is right now) or Snapchat, and instead of looking at ways to establish some boundaries, you turn away, sigh, and check out on your smartphone.

You may have a chronic tech issue if the main way to control your children's tech is to snatch the devices out of their hands while they curse, kick, scream, run away, or try to hit you. That's a "pure frustration" parenting move. That's a "lack of preparation" parenting move. That's a "you need to fill up your cup stat" and "make a new plan" parenting move. And I don't care how much of a patient, amazing, and positive parent you are, (almost) *every* parent has done or will do the "snatch the tech" move, so don't go down the guilt spiral. We just need to rein it in and see it as a last resort measure, as well as a sign that you need a plan.

You may have a chronic tech issue if there aren't any rules around technology in your house. You haven't discussed it with your partner, and you haven't read any data on kids and tech. You have purchased items like tablets, turned on the parental controls (or not, if you were me), and handed over the devices. You don't have hours of acceptable use, nor do you treat the tablet as yours and the children are *allowed* to use it (unless your child purchased it himself, but still . . . your house, your rules). Your tech rules boil down to the child just uses the tablet whenever he wants (which is all the time) and you scream about him getting off of it (which is also all the time).

You may have a chronic tech issue if you believe that apps, software, game blockers, and controls are going to parent your child for you. Okay, so at the time of publishing this book, I know that there are hundreds (if not thousands) of ways to block, prohibit, and slow your children's ability to be online and access scary stuff. I also know that, as soon as these apps and software hit the street, kids have found a way to crack them. I don't personally have anything against the apps and devices that control children's tech use; I think that they can do a world of good. *But* I have a lot of side-eye for the parents who buy all the tech safety apps and expect that these digital babysitters will control all things screen for them. No matter how sophisticated the program, nothing replaces the communication between a child and the parent. Part of the communication between parent and child is literally getting your children physically off the tech. There is no list or app that replaces some good ol'-fashioned parental nagging. Oh, I know, nagging is a big no-no in the Positive Parenting world, and do I want you to *only* nag? No. But is nagging part of parenting? Yes, and because you are often the only person in the house looking out for *anyone's* welfare, and when you have people who are actively working against their own interests, nagging is sadly required. I think of it like this: You know the speed limit of your regularly traveled highway, right? It is either 55, 60, or 65 mph. But the highway patrol still places signs along the road, still places cops in secret places with speedometers, and still uses neon signs that flash "Speed Kills, Slow Down." Nagging, nagging, nagging. Why do they do this? Because humans really cannot be trusted to our own devices and willpower. We are pretty bad at sticking to the rules, especially when our brains love fun and excitement and danger, real or perceived. So, yeah, parents, you need to get in there and nag your children to get them away from technology. Stop relying solely on contracts and apps to parent your children.

You may have a chronic tech issue if your child owns and breaks tech item after tech item, with little to no consequence. From flinging it in a fit of rage to dropping it while walking to the car, children break their devices. Cracked screens and spilled water on devices happen, but I have worked with more than a couple of families for whom replacing a device (with no inconvenience to the child) is a fairly regular occurrence. I really do believe that shit happens, and I absolutely think that there is a time and place to help your kids out. Mistakes are real and even the most responsible human makes them, but when I see a ten-year-old on his fourth tablet of the year? No. That's not okay. It says to me that your child isn't mature enough to handle that tablet, and the parent needs to take it back until the child matures a bit.

Also, I know you already know this, but we are doing a huge disservice to our children if we replace cracked screens, devices, and tablets without any sacrifice or loss to the children. It is not as though we are trying to actively punish our children; we just know that there is no greater lesson learned than the lesson of losing something you love. For children, no lecture, no contract, and no promise is a substitution for the pain of not having their device. Period. Allowing your child to experience the pain of losing a device, either permanently or for a period of time, creates a neural pathway that says, "When I throw my tablet around and it breaks, I lose it. This is the worst feeling in the world, and Dad was not kidding when he said he would take it away." If you want your child to appreciate the value of devices, don't keep replacing them.

But, before it gets to that point, step in and take control of where the device goes. You can say to your child, "I appreciate that you love your smartphone, and when you leave the house with it, you lose it. We are going to keep it here in the house because it is too expensive to keep replacing the phone." The yelling and denials and negotiating from the child will be epic, but there is no other way to help them understand the value of these small computers! While you may be angry that your child cannot take care of their devices, it is our parental responsibility to help them. This is especially true and kind for children with executive functioning issues! Their brains simply cannot hold on to their good intentions, so hoping that they will take care of their devices is not a parenting strategy that will work.

You may have a chronic tech issue if you hide your children's devices and technology throughout the house. Okay, true story: One summer, in a fit of rage over the abuse of tech in my house, I gathered every device I laid eyes on (a brand-new iPhone, an iPad Mini, and a Kindle) and placed them under a pile of dirty clothes in my bedroom. After about an hour, I scooped up these clothes and put them in the washer, popped in a detergent tablet, and hit the On button. (You see where this is going, right?) I heard *BANG CLANG BANG CLANG*, but thought, *Hmmm, that's weird. Must be a big zipper.* It was only when I went to put the clothes from the washer into the dryer that I realized what I had done. Forgetting I had hidden the devices in the laundry, I accidentally ran a load of tablets and smartphones. As I held the waterlogged devices in my hands, shock and shame filled my body, and I knew that no bag of brown rice that was going to fix this mess. Each screen was cracked and water dripped out of every angle. Oh my God, I had put all of my children's devices through a wash cycle because I had acted like a child myself.

Is it okay to, here and there, hide a tablet so that your child can get a grip and reenter reality? Sure. Hiding tech isn't child abuse and it is far from the worst thing you can do as a parent, but there will come a time when you hide a device and you will not be able to find it . . . and that, my friend, is the worst. My husband is guilty of hiding the TV remote from our girls, and there have been numerous times when I have not been able to watch my *Housewives* on the DVR due to this secret location. This is decidedly *not* okay. Not to mention, our children have a way of finding our hiding spots, and their sneakiness level can impress even a professional burglar. *And* a time will come when your children are using their devices for practical reasons, and hiding the device is simply not an option. "But, Mom, I am writing a paper!" will be the phrase you hear, even though you and the child both know that they have been watching *The Office* on Netflix for the last three hours.

Have I depressed you yet? Feeling like a total failure when it comes to the screens and your child? Well, good, you are in the same boat with the rest of us. No one—not the experts, not the neuroscientists, not the pediatricians, definitely not the tech sector, *no one*—really knows what is happening or what to do when it comes to children and tech, let alone adults and tech. The invention of handheld devices is too recent to fully understand their impact, but our common sense and intuition knows that chronically staring into a screen is not good for most children.*

Tech, social media, screens, gaming, and the like are here to stay, and we parents need to join together to accept the reality of these inventions, as well as their impact on our lives. Every family has the right to decide how and when tech will be used in their family, so let's support one another on this journey. Less judging, more support. Less worry, more confidence! And because this is a chapter about assessing if you have a problem with technology, I wanted to offer some concrete takeaways for you to ponder, journal on, and take or leave. Which of these ideas or solutions speaks to you the most? What can *you* do about tech and your family?

REFLECT AND WRITE

1.   What you pay attention to grows. You pay attention to your phone? You will just keep paying more attention to your phone. Ask yourself every day, "What or who got my eye contact today?" The same goes for your children. More time on devices usually equals *more time on devices*. Don't wait for your child to "grow out" of tech use; it isn't going to happen. You may have to work harder to find other things for your child to do, but it is worth it.

2.   Check your own tech habits, *then* feel confident bringing your children into line (see Chapter 9). If you look in the

---

* Of course there are children who learn and communicate best with and through technology, so please follow your intuition, as well as the recommendations of specialists, to best use technology in your family life.

mirror and know that you are checked out, get yourself straightened out first, *then* address the family needs. Kids can quickly sniff out a hypocrite, and they will not respond kindly to a screen crackdown by someone who cannot control their own impulses.

3. Establish some universal tech rules for the house. I know that you are busy, but there *are* many times in a day that everyone in the family can share a tech rule. Examples: No tech at the dinner table, no tech when there is family movie night (I have been called out many a time for "watching the movie" while scrolling, ouch), no tech when someone is sharing a story with you, no tech at family celebrations or parties, or no tech during certain car rides.

4. Yes, there are always exceptions (your work, their communication with a friend who is waiting on them, etc.), but everyone can find a way to agree on a certain set of rules. Your children will appreciate these efforts, even if they never tell you so. Especially if they never tell you so.

5. Accept that battling technology will be a never-ending battle. There is no "winning" the tech wars. Yes, you can take tech "fasts" or breaks (and I highly recommend them), but technology and devices are not going anywhere. In fact, they creep into our lives more and more, every single day. So, simply accept that this is now as much a part of your parenting life as healthy foods and good sleep and homework and vaccines. Is it fair? No, but life isn't fair and you didn't become a parent to make your life easier, so *buckle up.*

6.   Practice using good tech etiquette around your kids; it is powerful and it works. You may not see the results immediately, but you will begin to notice how often you are picking up your phone or glancing away from your child if you practice saying, "Pardon me . . ." each time you do. You will also begin to notice that what you *think* are "important needs" aren't really all that important after all. Either boredom or habit or a mix of both, our screen etiquette will keep us (hopefully) honest.

7.   If you have depression, anxiety, or another mental health issue, you will suffer more from social media and tech than the average person on the street. You don't need to swear off all devices; you just need to stay aware of your moods and screen usage. I strongly suggest finding someone to whom you can say, "Wow, I am spiraling," and make sure that person holds you accountable for your tech use. It may sound silly, but it really helps to know that there is someone out there who knows you are struggling and is supporting you.

CHAPTER 10

Your Child Doesn't Have to Be a Spoiled Bully, I Promise

For most of the time that children have walked the earth, there has been a "seen and not heard" kind of mentality surrounding them. Yes, every culture in the world has its own unique relationship with children, but for a vast majority of American history, children were largely (1) unavoidable (due to lack of birth control) and (2) needed to work as part of a family's agricultural lifestyle. Children and their needs were not considered vitally important, and while children were loved, they were not worshiped.

Fast-forward to today and, boy, has that changed.

Children are now glorified and placed upon a dangerously high pedestal. We are obsessed with our children: their happiness, their emotional well-being, their education, their activities, their clothes and toys, their friendships, their work ethic (or lack thereof), and their place in the world. And while we are now following our children around like zombies, attending to their every need, I want to make something crystal clear: The good ol' days were not so good. I mean, were children more independent? Yes, usually. Were children allowed more physical outside time? Yes, for sure. Were children allowed to be more bored, hence more creative? Yes, we can guess that without technology, their minds were a bit freer to wander. Were children less neurotic? Probably, but I am not going to build out a causality argument here re: parenting and anxiety.

But.

Children in the good ol' days were often the bearers of harsh discipline and beatings for being, well, regular kids. Children were largely ignored and, God forbid you had an emotional or physical problem, there was not much that was done to help you. Boys were expected to be manly and tough (this is changing . . . a bit too slowly) and not much was expected from girls at all, except child-rearing and domesticity (unless Dad was at war or otherwise gone, then all kids did all roles). The roles and rules in family life were largely clear, narrow, and inescapable.

So, the good ol' days may have been a "simpler time," with clearer rules for everyone to follow (meaning: white, straight men who had completely neurotypical children were doing A-OK), but I wouldn't want to raise children back then for anything.

But our American parenting culture has a way of swinging from one extreme to another, and I think we have all witnessed the very opposite of children being "seen and not heard" take root. Our children are heard and seen *all of the time*, even more seen and heard than we, the people who are supposed to be in charge of them! Consequently, a lot of our children are the bosses of us and they are (unconsciously) bullying us. Badly.

And lest you think my family has not succumbed to this bullying dynamic, think again. Over the last fifteen years, both my husband

and I have had multiple incidences where we run and hide when we even *hear* one of our children stomping down the stairs. My husband, in particular, has hidden behind couches and in bathrooms, and he has run out the front door of our home (and we live in a city, so there are people around), so bad was the wrath of our children. Can you imagine previous generations of fathers hiding from their children?

If this is a problem in your home, you are probably nodding right now. Here's a scenario that may appear in some of our homes:

Brett (*five*): I want some water.

Parent: How do you ask nicely?

Brett: Give me the water.

Parent (*sighing loudly and handing over the water*): Brett, we have talked about using our "pleases" and "thank-yous."

Brett: I want my Star Wars cup. This is not my cup.

Parent: That cup is in the dishwasher and . . .

Brett: I want my Star Wars cup *now*.

(*Voices are becoming louder.*)

Parent: This is all there is, sorry, Brett.

Brett: FIND MY CUUUUUPPPPP!

Parent: Brett, *stop screaming!* Do you want me to fish it out of the dishwasher? I am not doing that.

Brett: GET MY CUUUUUUUP. NOOOOOOOOOW!

Parent (*Opens running dishwasher and fishes out the cup, and rinses it while the cheap plastic burns her fingers.*): Brett, I am doing this for you once and once only. (*She also did it yesterday.*) I am tired of you telling me which cup you will use and which cup you won't. This is unacceptable, do you hear me? UN-ACCEPT-ABLE. (*Hands cup of water to Brett.*)

Brett (*Walks away.*)

END SCENE

A similar scenario may occur at your dining room table or in the child's room while they dress. It may be while you are putting them to bed or trying to walk away from the ice-cream truck. You get the point, right? The child is utterly in charge of the situation.

One of my children (who will remain nameless to protect their innocence) once demanded ice cream in the frozen-food aisle and when my husband said no, she flattened him with a punch to the nads. I mean, seriously. He was on the floor of Whole Foods, clutching his twig and berries, and our four-year-old stood over him cracking her knuckles like a mob boss. AND SHE GOT THE ICE CREAM. When I say I get it, I get it.

As a parent coach, I have had clients whose children dictate an entire family vacation. I have seen children decree which foods will be eaten in the house as well as when they will be eaten. I have witnessed children throw a sandwich on the floor (and the child is well beyond toddler age) and demand the parent remake the sandwich. I have seen children who dictate when they go to bed, when they use their technology, and when they have playdates.

"The children are *horrible*," the parents cry.

"The country is *ruined*," we weep.

"How will these children *cope*?" we worry.

But it's not the kids. It's *not* the kids, people. It's us. We cannot abdicate our authority and expect an immature person to handle that power well. Reflect on this. We have, in front of us, a small human who only recently learned to dress herself, yet we want her to realize she's being bossy, stop that bossiness, give us back the power, and say sorry for taking it in the first place? That is not going to happen.

So, in order to wrestle back the power required to guide your family, the number one issue you have to face is this: This is not your child's fault. Oh, listen. I have coached hundreds and hundreds of parents over the years, and I know how difficult some of our children can be. Born intense and extra sensitive, these children demand more of their parents than the average child. Certain children seem to be born with a supernatural sense of boundary pushing; their tenacity is a thing both to be feared and respected, and I know (from firsthand experience) that almost every parent in this world did not choose to let go of the reins. After twenty years of working with families, I have never met a parent who said, "You know, Meghan? One morning I just said, 'Screw it, I am too tired to care. I am going to allow my child to take over, disrespect me, boss me around, and generally become a mini Mussolini right in front of my eyes.'"

And in this vein, the fact that your child is a spoiled brat is also not your fault. True, there are some egregious examples (easily seen on reality TV) where we can witness parents giving their absolute best effort to create the absolute worst child, but mostly? There is a slow and steady progression of boundaries moved, ignored, and completely dropped; a consistent wearing down of the parental soul that seems to occur to these parents. Death by a thousand requests and whines sounds about right.

I don't believe, though, that we are doomed. For however child-obsessed we are, we are also an incredibly empathic, educated, compassionate, globally minded, and knowledgeable group of parents. We know more about what makes us and our children tick than any other generation of parents who has walked the earth (well, maybe). True, that knowledge doesn't seem to be helping us, but still, we are up to the challenge of helping our children be cooperative and kind!

The way to combat the bossiness isn't to double down and begin the punishing, punitive ways of the good ol' days, nor is it to cower in the corner and read and reread parenting books, hoping to find the perfect answer (this book being the exception, natch). No, we are not going for extremes. We are going for the middle way. The way of staying flexible and holding our boundaries. The way of knowing when to change our minds and when to toe the line. We can balance enthusiastic yes's and strong no's. We can understand that our children's frustration and bossiness is not a disorder and neither is our anger. We can make friends with our own parenting imperfections and foibles, and not be afraid of these imperfections. We can acknowledge when we have created patterns in our parenting lives that need to be looked at squarely and honestly. And above all, we can find the silver lining in our children's behavior (and they so desperately need that). Smart, balanced action is needed to help our children become less bossy as well as help us get back in the driver's seat.

Who's the Boss?

How do we understand and use our intuition to help our bossy, bratty, bullying, and beautiful children?

First, we must believe that our children are inherently good and *want* to be good for us. I can hear you now, "Meghan, you don't know my kid. He is pretty awful and he doesn't want to be good at all, trust me." And yes, I have had moments where I have looked at my own children and thought, "Nope, their souls are evil and there is no goodness in there." But the truth? True psychopathology is extraordinarily rare in children, and it is even more rare that children are just born truly "bad." There is almost always a mixture of nature and nurture at play that creates a child who lacks a conscience, and chances are preeeeetty good this isn't your kid, okay? (But, if for any reason you think that your child is displaying behaviors that deeply worry you, get yourself and the child to the pediatrician, stat.)

In asking you to believe that your children are inherently good, I am not trying to paint humans to be simplistic or without our faults and foibles. We are complicated and fallible mammals, quite controlled by our limbic system. We are prone to panic and making bad decisions based on that panic. We can be vengeful, jealous, petty, mean, spiteful, and weak. But let's remember, we are talking about children. Yes, they are immature and inclined to be hijacked by their emotions, but they are not carrying the same emotional baggage we parents do. Not even close. They haven't accumulated a lifetime of bad habits or emotional wounds, and their capacity to want to be good for their connections (loving parents) is real and true. Even the most defensive and angry child wants to be good; they just don't know how.

> # Even the most defensive and angry child wants to be good; they just don't know how.

Believing your child is inherently good is the first step in turning your own mind toward positive action, as well as helping your children become less bossy. If you awaken and assume that your child is bad *and* you are not up to the task, there will be no success. Also, working toward a negative goal—"I will make my child less awful"—won't work for obvious reasons. This is not Pollyanna thinking. At the Neufeld Institute, my teachers would say, "If you cannot see the good in your child, who will?" Who else is expected to offer unconditional love and hope *but* the parent?

How powerful is it to have someone you love believe in you? Let's look at a simple example, one that most of us have experienced at some point. Chances are good that you had a teacher whom you felt disliked you (I had scads of these teachers; in fact, I can only remember a couple of teachers who were kind to me . . .). Sure, you may have learned some facts from this teacher, but the truth? You were not inclined to work hard for that teacher. You didn't want to shine, to be your best self, to obey, to be in their good favor, or to make them happy. Why? We don't want to work hard for people who don't believe in us, and this is doubly true for our children. On the flip side, if you have had a teacher who deeply believed in you, thought you were a good person, a person worthy of respect and praise, you probably would have moved heaven and earth for that teacher. You gave it your all, not because you were smitten with the subject matter, but because you wanted to please this teacher! You wanted to be your best self. This is how powerful connection is for our children. We the parents must *believe* in their better angels. When we expect and fear the bullying behaviors, that's what we will end up getting; it is a self-fulfilling cycle of anger and defiance, with no end in sight.

We the parents must *believe* in their better angels.

This can all sound a bit confusing given how paradoxical parenting is. On the one hand, I am asking you to simply believe in the best parts of your children. I am not asking you to manufacture scenarios in which your child behaves better/properly/up to your expectations, *then* trust your child. Rather find the trust is there, right now! But on the other hand, I am also asking you to be forward-thinking. I want you to anticipate your children's thoughts and behaviors and handle them with calm and purpose; to stay aware *and* utterly cognizant of the past, how it is affecting the present, and how it may affect the future (when it comes to your children). I recognize that this can be confusing, but if you don't think about it too much, it makes total sense.

Another confusing aspect of bossiness is that it is developmentally appropriate for children to negotiate or disobey us. This disobedience is a sign of growth; it means that the child is learning her own mind. The child is developing her own opinions, likes, and dislikes, and this child wants to feel seen and heard in her family. Starting around two years of age, children challenge the system for years and years (decades, really), and this is completely in line with developmental growth. I repeat: This is utterly normal. But we parents assume that this natural pushback is "misbehavior." We are shocked, challenged, and frankly, scared of all this noise and upset. To stop the screaming, whining, begging, and demanding, we give in to the demands, and when we give in to the demands, we give up our power. This "push-shock-yell-give-up" dynamic causes a great deal of insecurity in the child. "Wait," their limbic system screams. "How come it is so easy to push Mom around? This isn't right . . ." And instead of backing down, the child takes the power (because someone has to), but none of this sits right with the child. Even though the child feels like he is pushing you around, *he doesn't want to be in charge*. It feels simultaneously powerful, awesome, and wrong.

It may sound confusing and paradoxical, and even though it *seems* like your child wants to be the boss, she doesn't. They desperately need and want you to be a compassionate and boundaried leader. If you have ever had the opportunity to know a true bully, you would see the misery just under the surface of their steely exterior. This child may have control of the teacher and most of their classmates, but after the bravado and blustering are stripped away, it is easy to see that the child is desperate for compassionate and, above all, strong leadership. All children want to be guided by a loving and strong parent; it is how our species flourishes. There is a strong hierarchy in humans, and children are not meant to be or stay in charge of their parents. Why would nature create a system where the immature would physically, emotionally, and intellectually run the show? Humans would've never made it this far! And here is the real irony for us parents: The more power your child gets, the more power they want. It is like sugar: even though too much sugar wreaks havoc on *all* of our bodily systems, our brain craves the hit. It feels so good. So, when Brett got the Star Wars cup (from the example above), his brain had a hit of "Winning!" and even though it gave him low-level insecurity, his power grabs keep going and growing.

> # All children want to be guided by a loving and strong parent.

Our parental instinct may want to punish the child out of this cycle, but if you currently have a bully in your house, you know that punishment doesn't work; in fact, it makes the behavior worse. No, we need a rational, steady, and experienced parent to hold the boundaries while employing language that uses more emotion and less logic.

Feelings First

The first step to reestablishing some control in your family is to stop using rational language to solve an emotional problem. If you have been in the habit of fighting with your child over who has the power or talking endlessly about the problem and how the child needs to improve, well, you have already discovered that the rational route is not going to work. Our children aren't lawyers (no matter how skilled they seem at negotiating) and are not able to follow all of our logic and mandates. Does Brett love the Stars Wars cup? Sure, it is a special cup, but explaining (over and over) why the cup isn't available is not going to satisfy Brett. A power-hungry kid wants what they want, and your dishwasher explanation ain't gonna cut it. You are bringing a rational weapon to an emotional battle. Not to mention, the back-and-forth conversation serves only to grow frustration and anger; both the parent and the child want the other to understand their needs, but to no avail. As the parent, it is our responsibility to stop the conversation on our end, as well as let go of expecting our children to care about our reasoning (for now). I promise, there will be a time when your child will care about logic, but for now? When you stop asking your child to care about your perspective, you will cut down on much of the back-and-forth that plagues your current relationship.

Another way to reestablish control of your house is to assume that your child has good intentions (as we mentioned), yet will surely forget all the promises they have made. You will make a sticker chart and do *all the things* to get Brett to stop harassing you. You will ask your children to sign sensible contracts and agree to judicious rewards and logical punishments. You will create complex and thoughtful lists of unacceptable behaviors with colorful markers, and you will explain the way the brain works to your child. You will teach them meditative breathing (the newest way that parents are trying to skip over the hard parts of parenting), and you will point out how the child's actions don't seem to make sense. Your child will agree with anything you say in the moment, nodding vigorously.

"Brett, you cannot yell at Mommy anymore. You have to listen to me when I tell you that you cannot have your cup. I am the mother, I am in charge."

Brett will agree and he will mean it! Truly, all of his good intentions are right there in that moment, but alas . . . when it comes time to "not yell at Mommy," in the moments of wanting the cup? He has long forgotten that promise because, first, Brett mostly lives in the present moment, and second, old habits die hard. The insecurity and the habit of taking back the power kicks in, hence all of his well-intentioned promises vanish into thin air, like they were never made to begin with. This is maddening for parents, but if you know this "forgetting" is coming, you won't take it personally. You won't double down on your punishments; you will understand that it takes an immature mind some time to accept a new way of doing things. And you will understand that talking about logic-based solutions without first focusing on your children's emotions will almost always lead you to the same place: nowhere.

So, if the child is an emotional creature (a given) and he is drunk on power, is it easy to establish a balance and regain some of the power you have lost? Welp, I am not going to lie . . . it is hard. Nothing makes me sigh more than when I read a book or a column or a blog that tosses off "three easy ways to get your child to stop being a little Napoleon." (Meanwhile, I may have written that exact column, and if I have, forgive me.) Puleeeze. If it were that easy to make your child kindly obey you, you would have done it already! No, facing down your child's bullying behaviors is like facing down Hydra. Every time you try to create and enforce a boundary, the child grows another way to bully and subvert your power. This is both daunting and depressing, and I don't want to paint it as easy or fun. The longer your child has bossed around you and your family, the longer it may take to wrestle back the reins, but there *is* a way through. We are going to focus on the *emotions* underneath the bossy surface of your child's difficult behavior.

Using Emotional Language

The easiest and simplest way to tap into your child's emotional life and begin to unspool their need to bully is to begin a sentence with, "It sounds like . . ." or "It sounds like you feel . . ." and insert any feeling word that seems to fill the bill. The beautiful thing about children is that they are happy to correct you when you are wrong about their emotions. Here is how the Brett situation may play out if you use emotion rather than passive-aggressive logic:

Brett: I want the Star Wars cup or I am not drinking the water.

Parent: I get it. It sounds like you really love that cup.

Brett: Yes, and it is all I will use. I will only drink from the Star Wars cup.

Parent: Huh. It sounds like you are dedicated to using that cup, no matter what.

Brett: Yes. Now give it to me.

Parent: I cannot do that, and I imagine that will make you feel pretty disappointed.

Brett: Yes, now get it.

Parent: I cannot do that, and I think you will feel frustrated by that.

Brett: MOOOOOOOOOOOOOM! (*Whining begins or crying or tantrum throwing.*)

Parent (*Stays silent while Brett throws himself on the floor and he swears to never drink water again. Brett eventually wears himself out and takes the cup of water initially offered, looking as sad as a child ever has.*)

END SCENE

You may be confused why the above scenario is better than punishment or giving in. Every parent I have ever met wants a strategy or parenting technique that results in peace, and I don't blame them! But as I like to say to my coaching clients, "There is suffering in the service of change and progress, and there is suffering for nothing but the sake of suffering." Yes, Brett ends up having a full-blown tantrum, but there is some good stuff happening here. Allow me to explain.

Tears That Heal

Remember: When Brett is pushing your boundaries around and gets the cup he wanted, he is filled with anxiety, despite the fact he is getting what he wants. His yelling and screaming result in a lose-lose for both of you, as we have already discussed. But the tears that come after you hold the boundary? *These are different.* Here is what's happening: As Brett's brain pushes and pushes his agenda forward, his frustration is increasing. As we peacefully hold the boundary, his frustration will eventually reach a breaking point where there is nothing left to do but cry about what he cannot change. As Dr. Gordon Neufeld says, "What you cannot change changes *you*." To sum it up, this *is* what resilience looks like when it is happening in real time. While exhausting, annoying, and heartbreaking, Brett breaking down in tears over his lack of a cup is a sign that his brain has grown a tiny neural pathway that says, "When Mom says she cannot get the cup, I don't get the cup." This is profound, this idea of his brain changing simply because you held a peaceful boundary. And a million little moments like this add up to Brett accepting that life will not always go his way, and my heavens, we need humans to get that, right?

You may be wondering how this idea (holding peaceful and strong boundaries that bring your bossy child to tears) relates to the chapter where I suggest that you go out like Jerry Seinfeld (exiting difficult scenarios with strength and grace). And yes, this is nuanced, so let's walk it out a bit. In this chapter, we are holding a boundary using calm and emotional language, bringing Brett to his eventual tears and acceptance. In the case of going out with strength and grace, we may *decide* to give Brett the cup. It might sound like this:

> **The Scene:** Hosting all of your in-laws for Thanksgiving at your
> house (or any other situation, jam-packed with stress).

> **Brett:** Mom, I want a water.
> **Parent** (*Fills a red cup with water and hands it to him.*)
> **Brett:** Mom, I want my Star Wars cup.
> **Parent** (*Pauses and assesses her reality. She has to make the gravy,*
> *her father-in-law won't stop complaining about the beer*
> *supply, and her spouse is nowhere to be found. She decides to*
> *fish the Stars Wars cup out of the dishwasher, rinse it off, and*
> *hand it to Brett.*)
> **Parent:** Brett, I have decided that you should have your Star
> Wars cup; it's a special day. Go show it to Grandmom,
> OK? (*She smiles widely, confident in this decision.*)
> **Brett** (*Smiling, takes his cup and is off to find Grandmom.*)
> END SCENE

Did the parent give in to Brett's command? Yes and no. I am less concerned about the cup and more concerned with who has the *power* in the scenario. Though the parent decided that Thanksgiving was *not* the time to hold a boundary with little Brett, she is still completely in charge of the situation. Brett is not browbeating her, nor is he screaming or threatening her. When it is not Thanksgiving, when the in-laws are not lingering in the kitchen watching the gravy bubble, when the scenario is not already rife with anxiety, the parent can *choose* to hold the boundary and allow Brett to cry his sweet little face off. And yes, children can handle different responses to the same scenario.

My hope is that as you continue to focus on emotions and not just rational thought, the child will be able to eventually say something like, "I am really upset because I love that cup. There's just something special about it, and I am sad I cannot have it." I know that this may sound like a pie-in-the-sky interaction, but trust me, the more that *you* are able to kindly and strongly hold your boundary, the more your children will be able to cry about what they cannot change. Yes, it is painful to watch our children cry; it doesn't bring any caring parent pleasure to watch their children suffer and cry, but this is how humans adapt, become resilient, and hence, less bossy. And so, while we don't want to force our children to cry all of the time, we do want them to be able to feel sadness and use more emotional language. And the more you are able to use emotional language, the more likely that your children will become adults who can access their own feelings, have compassion for others, and communicate peacefully with all other humans. The practice, patience, and persistence required from us to hold the boundaries and use emotional language? It can be tough, and depending on how you were raised and your own emotional literacy, this can feel like a tall order. But bit by bit, you will find your own way to emotionally connect with your child.

The change toward using more emotion-based language may look like this:

1. You first realize and admit that you are stuck in a *rational* rut with your bossy child, and it isn't working.

2. You catch yourself using *logic* language over and over, and you are shocked at how much you actually do it. You can

actually watch the words tumble out of your mouth, even as you try to stop it. Old habits die hard, right?

3. You make a plan to change. You hang up sticky notes, practice phrases in the mirror, etc.

4. You try to use emotional language and feel like a total fake. Your anger is simmering right below your tight smile, your child sniffs out that something is different, and she doubles down in her bullying and bossiness.

5. You become irate and decide the emotional language stuff is for wimps, curse my name, and double down in your punishments to show that child who is boss.

6. You explode on your child and feel like total crap. The fights and power struggles worsen, and you remember why the rational and punishment stuff didn't work to begin with, and you go back to Step 1.

7. You begin to seriously practice your emotional language and voilà! Some hours, days, weeks, or months later, you begin to see glimmers of hope. Your child is having fewer tantrums and communicating more. Nothing is perfect, but the communication is better. And better is quite refreshing. You are proud, and best of all, you like your child a little more.

It is important to note that if your child is truly bossy, you cannot hold *all of the boundaries all of the time.* If you take this strategy and decide to go full tilt on all the boundaries, it is going to do a number on your relationship with your child. That is simply too much stress on an already tenuous relationship. Again, it isn't the child's fault that you dropped boundaries, so it isn't reasonable for you to go hog wild now that you have seen the truth of the dynamic. Choose the times that *you* can handle the whining and tears. Slow and steady is better than the scorched-earth approach.

Let's review why children become so bossy, and how we can help them unspool this tough dynamic. Our children are developmentally meant to challenge our commands (some more than others), and as they push, we drop our boundaries to sidestep the whining, crying, violence, begging, nagging, and harassment. We just want them to *stop*. As we chronically drop our boundaries, the child becomes increasingly insecure due to the flip in the roles of who should have the power in the family. The more insecure the child, the more power grabs they make, creating a never-ending cycle of bossiness. The parent is at their wits' end, but punishments and challenges to their power result in worsening behavior. But if we decide to judiciously and peacefully hold our boundaries, we will bring the child to the tears they so desperately need. These tears signify that their brain has accepted that life is not going their way, and *that's okay*. All of this is tough work, but well worth it. And remember: the bossier the child, the less you double down on every issue. Even the most intense children were not born to bully you. Yes, parenting them is hard, and yes, you are going to have to grow up in ways you never saw coming, but the alternative is suffering on top of suffering. It is worth holding the boundaries and allowing the tears to fall. It is worth it.

REFLECT AND WRITE

1.   How were the boundaries enforced when you were a child? Does that impact you today?

2.   Of the many times your child may bully you during an average day, choose one or two instances where you can calmly hold a boundary, practicing your emotional language. These times that you practice holding a boundary should not include when you feel rushed, fatigued, or distracted with other tasks. (I know this can feel daunting, but you *can* find at least one time.)

3.   Are you ready for this practice (using emotional language and assuming the best of your child) to be a lifelong practice? Are you ready to assume full responsibility for your own behavior, and forgive yourself when you make mistakes (mistakes are guaranteed)?

4.   Do you believe that your child is inherently good?

CHAPTER 11

Forcing Feelings onto Your Children Is Never Going to Work

I was recently at Disney World and I won't lie: I loved it. Yes, it is crazy-consumerist and too crowded, but my children were delighted, and so I delighted in them. I rode roller coasters with my arms up and screamed my face off. I didn't think about the presidency or climate change or anything else distressing. I just laughed and laughed. Pure freedom.

You might be guessing that I am going to write about the horrors of parenting I witnessed at Disney, stories of children getting spanked and shamed, yanked around and shouted at. But no! I mostly saw loving parents helping overwhelmed children. There were plenty of crying children, for sure, but I saw parents taking them to quiet corners and speaking to them in gentle tones. There were hugs, smiles, and lots of patience despite the heat and sensory overload. In fact, I marveled at the parenting I witnessed at Disney. Families of every stripe and type, from every country and background, all of them using their own unique love language for their children. It was a beautiful symphony, truly.

I was especially impressed by a family in the Orlando airport, who had a very tall six- or seven-year-old boy in the midst of an epic tantrum. From my standpoint, it appeared he had some sensory issues and the parents were clearly accustomed to these outbursts. He clung to his mother's leg and screamed something about an injustice perpetrated by his younger brother (apparently hits were also exchanged). I watched a calm come over the mom's face and she stood stock-still, holding two scalding coffees. The husband ran to her aid, gently peeled the boy off of her (which made his screaming worse). I began to panic, fearing that the father would berate him right there in the airport, but instead he led his son to a seat, got on his level, and started speaking quietly to him. The boy was literally screeching, and I could only imagine the father's embarrassment, but he did not even look up to see if anyone was watching them. He began to instruct the child to count his breaths, and soon the boy was simply crying about his brother; the screeching had subsided.

The father just hugged him and waited. No consequence was given, nor was the boy forced to apologize to his little brother. The boys settled down and ate some breakfast. All was calm again.

Ah, I thought. *What a wise father. He knows that the forced apology will incite more anger . . .*

What a master lesson in parenting, right? I spent the flight reflecting on what would have happened if he had forced his son to apologize. Certain disaster, that's what would have happened. I can imagine that some of the people witnessing this outburst wanted the screaming child to be harshly reprimanded and made to apologize to this brother, but this would have backfired horribly.

Why?

Whether we force our child to apologize or force them to admit they were wrong or force them to appreciate our point of view, *forcing feelings* will always lead to an equal and opposite reaction from our children. Humans, especially children, are allergic to being told how to feel, and coercing a child into guilt or compassion will only lead to frustration and struggle.

> *Forcing feelings* will always lead to an equal and opposite reaction from our children.

When we demand apologies, we are parenting from a place of control and anger. And worst of all, we are training our children to say things they don't mean. We don't give true remorse, sorrow, and guilt a chance to occur naturally. So, if we cannot force empathy in our children, how can we get a child to feel sorrow?

First, the ability for your child to feel empathy depends a great deal on their age, so you need to understand the norms of your child's age. For instance, the average two-year-old has one perspective: their own. The extent to which they can feel remorse is limited greatly by the very fact that their outlook is extraordinarily narrow, and this is absolutely on track for the age. For a two-year-old, the sun rises and sets with their attachments, and while two-year-olds have big hearts, they cannot walk in your shoes. So, to coerce a two-year-old into sharing or saying sorry is a fool's errand. The hardest part about accepting this reality is that you have to combat the ever-present fear that beats like a drum:

If I don't teach my child to share, she won't learn how to share.

If I don't teach my child to be sorry, she won't ever care about hurting people.

If I don't nip this in the bud, my child will grow up to be a serial killer.

If you can accept that young children (usually five and under) struggle with caring about others' feelings as much as they care about their own, you will save yourself a world of grief. It is not as if these feelings of empathy and compassion aren't coming; they are! You just need to push Pause on the belief that you can force them to emerge.

Once you understand what is typical for your child's age, you need to match that against the actual child you have in front of you. Since each child is different, you should tailor your expectations to suit your specific child. For instance, I have a daughter who was born with her heart on her sleeve. Once when she was four, she watched an elderly man cross the street, and because he was totally hunched over, he moved very, very slowly. I heard a little sniffle, and when I looked down at her, she had tears streaming from her eyes. Alarmed, I immediately asked what was wrong. She pointed her chubby little finger at the elderly man and just said, "It is really hard for him, Mommy." Did I (or do I) need to force empathy from her? No, in fact I often needed to protect her from movies and situations that were too emotional (and trust me, that can get exhausting), as well as protect her from apologizing for issues that weren't her fault.

On the other hand, I have had many a client whose gifted children struggle with emotionally relating to others, and these children are nine, ten, and eleven years old. By developmental standards, these children *should* care about the interior worlds of others, but the wiring of their brains is slowing that down a bit. It doesn't mean that empathy isn't *ever* present; it just means that their compassion muscle needs a little more exercise. Many children have rigid thinking ("I am right; he is wrong"), and while they may be able to run circles around other children in math, for instance, their ability to feel sorrow may need a bit more time to develop.

In either case, whether you have a child who feels too much or feels too little, you cannot rush nature, but once you have a grip on your child's developmental and personal growth (see the resources in the back of this book for more information), you can make a suitable plan for your child to exercise their empathy muscle. What are some easy ways to help your child find their empathy?

- **Do not demand remorse in the moment of upset or turmoil.** I don't care how old your child is, if they have hurt someone and aren't ready to say sorry, do not force it *in the moment*. The blowback isn't worth it. And if you question this advice, imagine how you would feel if your spouse or friend rudely demanded you apologize to the person you upset? You might feel ashamed or angry, but you wouldn't feel sorry, that's for sure. When children are upset, their ability to think rationally is simply not there, and demanding remorse only lengthens the amount of time it will take for the brain to reach equilibrium. This is true for children of all ages.

- **When it comes to remorse and empathy, time is your friend.** I am not a neuroscientist and I don't play one on TV, but here's the breakdown: When you are super pissed, upset, or livid, your prefrontal cortex is like how my internet service so often is: temporarily unavailable. Our brains and hormones are working together to protect us from danger, and this results in a momentary shutdown of the thoughtful part of our brain. Our brain does this because we cannot run or fight or play dead and *think* about it too much; that would mean certain failure. No, our ability to be judicious gets shut down in the service of the larger needs, even if those needs aren't actually threatening us! But when our children have a moment to breathe, be alone, stomp it off, or go scream it out, the brain begins to slowly come back to itself. And if we don't bully or push or threaten, remorse will emerge. This brain stuff? This is how every human is built. Time is your friend, parent. If you feel an apology must be made in the moment, make it on behalf of the child.

- **When time has passed, test the compassion waters.** Does your child feel ready to talk about what happened? Can you assess where they are in their emotions? When the feelings have settled, it is appropriate to say, "Whoa, buddy. That was a lot, huh? How do we feel about what went down?" And then get quiet and listen. It is absolutely fine to say something like, "I get why you were so mad, *and* what you said to your brother was completely out of line. We are going to have to make amends," and see how your child responds. If they sigh, that's your green light to proceed with ideas about some form of an apology (a note, a picture, saying it, etc.). If your child balks and is utterly outraged, then back off and recognize that continuing

with this line of questioning is not going to get you
where you want to go.

- **In the quiet moments, model what empathy
  looks like in *your* daily life.** From children's books to
  stories about your job to events in the news to your own
  childhood memories, there are plenty of ways to engage
  in thoughtful conversation with even your youngest
  child. The key is to not "think" for your child. Keep your
  musings open-ended by saying things like, "I wonder
  how that little kitten felt when she lost her mitten? Do
  you think she felt sad?" Or "Malala is so brave. Do you
  think she gets nervous to speak to huge groups of people?
  How do you think she stays courageous?" Or "I
  remember hurting my best friend's feelings, it was hard
  to say sorry . . ." or "When I was younger, I was a
  nervous wreck before every baseball game. Sometimes I
  even wanted to cry . . ." If you don't push the child to
  give you the "right answer," you make space for the
  empathy wheels to begin to turn in their own minds.

- **Acknowledge that empathy and compassion are
  not static.** It isn't as though one minute we are devoid
  of compassion and then boom! We are compassionate.
  An evolving human never stops learning about the
  world and its suffering, and a child is only at the
  beginning of this journey. It isn't natural to expect a
  child to be able to appreciate the world's suffering; they
  are struggling to understand themselves day to day!
  When you worry, as a parent, that your child doesn't
  seem to care about others, remember that (God willing)

your kid has a long life ahead of them, full of twists and turns, joys and sorrows. Life will shape them in ways you cannot imagine; your job is to ready them for the journey, not create the journey.

- **When in doubt, focus on connecting with your child.** The flip side of sorrow is joy, so if you can experience moments of joy and happiness with your child, there is the greater likelihood that the child can feel remorse. Connection brings about emotional safety in children, and when a child feels safe, they can make room for others' perspective. Ask any child in juvenile detention who they care about, and they will respond, "No one, because no one cares about me." Because attachment and connection are the paths to everything good in our lives, remember that it is your primary tool for helping your child care about others. Doubt this? Find interviews of the most compassionate people the world has seen; they will speak of others who loved them dearly. Family, teachers, strangers who brought them joy and a feeling of belonging. It is powerful, this connection stuff.

Resist shaming your child into empathy and compassion.

If you do nothing else on this, don't be a pusher. Your in-laws, your mother, your neighbors, well-meaning teachers, many other people will try to shame you into shaming your child. Resist shaming your child into empathy and compassion. Guilt is not remorse. Pity is not compassion. Connect, connect, connect. Have faith, have faith, have faith.

REFLECT AND WRITE

1. Can you identify situations where you may be pushing your children into feeling remorse? What has happened as a result of that pushing?

2. Can you have faith that remorse and compassion will *emerge* in your children?

3. Can you think of three ways to communicate or model remorse and compassion in simple and authentic ways?

CHAPTER 12

Is It Too Late Now to Say Sorry?

I was a fortunate child in many respects, and one of the ways that good fortune manifested was that I had a mother who would apologize to me after we battled. Like many mothers and daughters, we could go a couple of rounds as I reached my tween and teen years. Voices were raised, some cereal boxes may have been thrown, and doors were slammed so hard the hinges would rattle. Inevitably I would be lying on my bed, wishing my mother was dead, when she would come in and sit next to me. With tears in her eyes, she would apologize for losing it on me. Even though I had screamed terrible things at her and even though I may have deserved much worse than I got, *she* apologized to *me*. She never once said, "Meghan, if you hadn't . . ." or "Meghan, you made me . . ." She simply apologized for her part in the argument. And even though I imagined that I still hated her in that moment, my mother role-modeled something very important: the power of a *sincere* apology. It left an indelible imprint on me, and I am more likely to apologize to my own children because of it.

Did you know that the roots of the word "apology" are *apo-* ("away from, off") and *logia* (from *logos*, meaning "speech")? According to Merriam-Webster's, the word's earliest meaning was "something said or written in defense or justification of what appears to others to be wrong or of what may be liable to disapprobation." This is funny because it is, in essence, the politician's apology! This early meaning essentially says an apology is saying, "I am sorry if you took my insult to heart, and here is why the insult still fits . . ." That's a phony apology, according to today's standards. Ironically, if my mom wanted to literally apologize to me, she would have listed the reasons she had lost her temper with me and, furthermore, insisted she very much had the right to do so! And while it seems that no one is sure when the word "apology" turned into actual regret and sorry (the "I am sorry" we know today), we definitely know when someone apologizes in the original, politician-like way, don't we? When someone gives us an "I am sorry, but if you hadn't been such a jerk, I would not have been so rude," well, we know that apology doesn't feel too great. We don't want to hear someone defend themselves, blame us for their bad behavior, and dress it up as an apology.

And yet, how often do you think parents give the crappy apology to their kids? Too often.

Our children can sniff out a fake apology faster than you can say "Justin Bieber." Before the apology has even fallen out of our mouths, they know that it is a passive-aggressive way to blame them for our own bad behavior. Some of our fake apologies may sound like this:

> *"I am sorry you are crying, but I told you 'no' about a hundred times."*

"I am sorry you are mad, but you knew we were getting a gift for your friend at the toy store, not for you."

"I am sorry you fell off of your bike, but I told you not to ride it until I was outside with you."

"I am sorry I yelled, but you push me right to the edge, every day."

You don't have to be a rocket scientist to see what links these bad apologies: It is the "but." Whenever you apologize and then "but" yourself, you have negated whatever it is you have just said. For some parents, the faux apology represents their true effort to try to make their kid feel better. They believe, despite all evidence to the contrary, that their children will hear them if the sentence begins with "I am sorry," and that somehow the children will ignore the glaring "but" in the middle of the apology. Parents assume that their children will really think they are sorry, but nope. Your children are not buying what you are selling.

Many parents also believe the fake apology is a little bit of sugar to help the medicine go down. For instance, if the parent says, "I am sorry you cannot have the cookie, but you knew you had to eat all your dinner to get it." In this example, the medicine is the fact that the cookie is not getting eaten, and the apology is supposed to be the sugar to help the child *understand* this reality. This apology (the kind meant to teach a lesson while simultaneously making the child feel better) is passive-aggressiveness at its best. And while I respect what the parent is trying to accomplish, I know for sure that the child does not appreciate the effort (as evidenced by the child's crappy behavior after this fake apology).

Some parents use "I am sorry, but" because they really think it is genuine and don't know how to do anything else. Maybe they grew up with poor apologies or maybe they really don't understand how fake it all sounds and how angry it makes their children. Or maybe the parent really *is* sorry, but it simply feels too vulnerable to sincerely apologize without the "but . . ." Think about it! If the "but" negates the apology, then the parent never has to face what he or she has really done; it is like dipping your toe into the sorry waters without diving into the deep end of the vulnerability pool.

Whatever the reason the parent inserts the "but" into the apology, it almost always makes the situation worse. I have never met a human (adult or child) who responds well when blamed for another's outburst. In an apology, you either completely own your actions, thoughts, and words, or you don't. If you feel justified in telling your child off or yelling or being unkind, then don't say you are sorry. You need to do some other therapeutic work stat, but don't muddy the waters with apologies that you don't mean or you feel forced to say.

Sorry-ish

"Wait, Meghan," you may be thinking. "Are you saying that I must feel 100 percent sorry every single time I apologize to my children?" Errrrrm, no. Not exactly. I mean, if I *only* apologized when I felt 100 percent sorry, I may not ever apologize to anyone ever again. So, when is it okay to apologize to your children when you aren't actually sorry?

Let me give you an example. When my eldest daughter eye rolls me for the fifty-eighth time and I snap, "Your damn eyes are gonna fall out of your head, you're rolling your eyes so hard, so knock it off!" I really mean it in that moment. Not even "kind of" mean it. I really want her to knock it the hell off. Even though I know better, and even though I know that she's in the midst of her crazy, hormonal teen life, there is just something about that fifty-eighth eye roll that hit me the wrong way (due to my own fatigue, hormonal imbalance, low blood sugar, lack of sunshine, whatever) and I snapped. Even after we take a break and I walk the dog and breathe and text my friend how much I hate parenting, I still don't feel all that sorry for snapping at her. The adolescent in me feels justified for my response to her. The immature me is saying, "Well, when I was her age, I would've had my face smacked for that many eye rolls, so she's getting off easy." The tween in me is saying, "WHATEVER." But the adult in me knows that I was out of line and I am responsible for my own words. So, despite the fact I am not feeling all that remorseful, I will say, "I apologize for snapping at you," and leave it at that. She may or may not forgive me, which is fine; I am not in charge of her emotions. The point is that as soon as I can muster up any kind of real humility, I will always apologize. Am I absolutely, positively, 100 percent sorry for how I spoke to her? Meh. Nah. Not really. But! I am the adult. This is my job. It is my role to see through my anger and frustration, and to find a way to demonstrate that, no matter what my children may have done, I don't get to be unkind and *also* give a fake apology. Essentially, it is my job to feel two feelings at once: my frustration with how hard it is to patiently raise children *and* the need to stay in control of my emotions and words. My child and I are not the same; we don't both get to spout off on one another and then not apologize when we are angry. I am the one that has to do better.

And yes, this is hard work.

For those of us who have come to maturation later in our lives (me), accepting this level of responsibility for my thoughts, words, and deeds is tiring work. Giving a true apology (or as close to a true apology as I can) takes a level of vulnerability that is highly threatening to our nervous systems. My panic is shouting, "If I say sorry to *her*, how will *she* ever learn *her* lesson? No, Meghan, you are *justified* in your righteous anger!"

Your fear may be shouting other things that keep the true apologies at bay, such as:

"If I say sorry, I will look weak in front of my children."

"If I say sorry, this gives my children a free pass to act like assholes for the rest of their lives."

"If I say sorry, this child will walk all over me."

"If I say sorry, I will start to cry."

"If I say sorry, I don't know what I will do next."

"If I say sorry, then I cannot punish this child."

"If I say sorry, I may never stop saying sorry. I am screwing up all the time."

This apology stuff is deep waters, emotionally speaking, because all of parenting is deep waters. Everything you fear in parenting is either an invitation to grow or an invitation to get stuck, so of course apologizing feels threatening.

Can you apologize to your children too much? Of course you can. If you apologize too often, you probably know who you are already. Whereas parents who resist apologizing tend to dig in, never ever say sorry to their children, and think that this is perfectly acceptable; the inverse is that there are parents who say sorry a million times a day, and often feel badly about how often they say sorry on top of that! These parents (who apologize too often) appear to be apologizing for simply existing and holding the most basic of parental boundaries.

They appear wishy-washy, scared, uncertain, and passive-aggressive. Underneath all this sorrow and hand-wringing, there is usually a parent who is simmering with resentment and fatigue. This parent usually wants to scream, "Screw it!" and really unload on their family, but they simply cannot. Or they *think* they cannot. The overapologist parent needs as much help as the parent who refuses to apologize. Either extreme fails to serve both the parent and child.

I know that it is easy to go down the spiral of "perfect parenting" and expect greatness from yourself, but that is not what is necessary here. Even when you make fumbling attempts at better apologies, a couple of amazing things happen when you attempt authentic apologies:

> *You show your child that it is okay to be frustrated.*

> *You show your child what emotional responsibility looks and feels like.*

> *You show your child what a true apology sounds* and *feels like.*

> *You set a blueprint for how your child gives and receives apologies (which is a super-duper big deal).*

> *And you show that you can reboot your moment or day with an apology.*

Each of these points is important, but let's take a closer look at that last one, shall we?

The power to use an apology to reboot your moment or day with your child is, quite simply, life-changing. And I am not suggesting we use this as a tool of manipulation; we are not just trying to move your child along or tossing off a quick apology to get a child to shut up. No, when a parent *decides* to let something go, forgive themselves, apologize, and move forward, it is like sprinkling magic over the whole family. Many parents I coach don't realize that they have this power: the power *to let shit go*. Which shit? Your own shit! You yelled because your four-year-old child threw himself on the ground in a tantrum, and when you went to comfort him, his foot came into contact with your boob. You let out a yelp and then yelled at him to "Watch your feet!" Scared, your son only cried harder while you sat there in pain, anger, and fatigue. You have a choice! After your brain comes back to itself, you can either declare that the day is "completely over" and throw in the towel, or you can see that an apology will right many wrongs here. "I am sorry I yelled and scared you. When you accidentally kicked me, it hurt." Maybe your son will understand you, maybe he won't, but isn't it enough to forgive yourself and move on? Isn't it enough to admit your humanity and say what needs to be said? Isn't it amazing to show your son that you understand him *and* you can apologize without punishing him? Yes, yes, and yes.

A funny thing happens when you regularly take responsibility for yourself and apologize for your missteps: Your child begins to trust you. As long as you are not abusing your ability to apologize and using it to manipulate your child, your child will see and feel your sincerity. They will witness what it is to be fully human: flaws, deep love, and all. Think of how powerful this is, of how this could affect their relationships with their friends, their future partners, and their co-workers! Think of the pain that could be lessened in this world if people could offer and receive a true apology. Without sounding hokey, effective and sincere apologies could change the entire world. No pressure.

Rupture, Meet Repair

When I think about apologizing to my own children, I often think of Dr. Dan Siegel. In his book *Parenting from the Inside Out*, he spends some time on the importance of "rupture and repair" in the parent and child relationship. There are many, many ruptures, disagreements, missed cues, miscommunication, and hurt feelings in all human relationships, and the fact that children are inherently immature causes even more day-to-day rupture. Add to this any significant life stressors and transitions, and you have opportunities for rupture all over the place! The most aware, awake, mindful, and knowledgeable parents have ruptures with their children; *it is the human parenting experience.*

What is the repair after the rupture? The repair is the acknowledgment of your parenting misstep, the apology to whomever deserves it, and your willingness to change your habitually problematic ways.

Rupture, repair. Rupture, repair.

It sounds so simple, but like all things in life, what appears to be the simplest task is often the hardest work, and a part of this seemingly simple repair process is that the parent should never wait for the child to apologize *first.* And after coaching hundreds and hundreds of parents, I have noticed that, either knowingly or unknowingly, parents are waiting for their children to have remorse first. These parents are withholding their own apology, waiting on their immature children to be the bigger person, and this expectation creates a hot, hot, hot mess in families. Trust me. The parents are unconsciously creating a dynamic that says: "I will say sorry to my child when I see that he is sorry for hurting me."

Inevitably, when I point out this dynamic to parents, they see it clear as day. "Oh my!" they exclaim. "I am being completely unreasonable!" I bow my knowing head and whisper, "My work here is done." But some parents will stick to their irrational guns, no matter what. "No, Meghan, my child needs to learn that he cannot get away with hitting his sister. If he doesn't apologize and mean it, he cannot go trick-or-treating!" I get it; I know how badly we parents would love to get true remorse from our children. (Check out Chapter 11 for more about remorse.) Despite the fact that I should know better, I am not immune to this desire. When I am tired and stressed-out, I too feel like I deserve the apology *first*. I want *them* to be better, to do better, to show me the respect I deserve. I get it.

But read this aloud: *Never ever, ever wait for your child to be more mature than you.*

Say it again: *Never ever, ever wait for your child to be more mature than you.*

Don't wait for the four-year-old, the eight-year-old, the eleven-year-old, the fifteen-year-old; don't wait for any of them to show more maturity than you. Don't withhold love and compassion while you wait for their remorse. Don't judge their entire character on their apology (or lack thereof). Developing your child's compassion muscle comes through kindness, patience, and strong boundaries—never through shame.

Even if your child is gifted with words and appears to be like an old man, so wise is his little brain . . .

Even if your child is fifteen and seems to have all of life figured out . . .

Even if your child "knows better" and you have already "worked through all of these issues ages ago with the play therapist" and "these shenanigans should be over by now" . . .

Even if, even if, even if.

You step up first. Every single time.

I found that when I just accepted this mandate (Don't expect your child to apologize first), it was easier for me to simply give the apology that I needed to give.

Justin Bieber asked the crucial question: "Is it too late now to say sorry?" And the answer is no. No, it is not. It is also not too late to give an apology that encourages connection, trust, and growth. It isn't too late to give up the "I am sorry, but . . ." It isn't too late to notice if you apologize all the time, for no good reason. And now is the time to take total responsibility for your own thoughts, behaviors, and emotions.

REFLECT AND WRITE

1. Was apologizing a sign of weakness in your family of origin?

2. Did your family of origin use apologies as a form of manipulation or were you shamed for vulnerability, showing emotion, tears, and/or feelings?

3. What are your apology habits when it comes to your children? Do you never apologize or apologize too much? Are you right in the middle?

4. Find a quiet moment and take the time to give your child an apology for a very recent misstep. No "buts" and no blaming. Just a good, sincere apology. Reflect on how it went and how you might do it next time.

CHAPTER 13

Your Parenting Techniques Aren't Working, Are They?

As I have mentioned many times, I have three children. When my youngest, Gigi, was eight, she was strong-willed, funny, smart, and alas, struggling with being the youngest. As a way to ease her worries, Gigi visited her school counselor numerous times (Ms. O), and there Gigi learned an interesting technique to manage her anger. Ms. O asked Gigi to imagine that she has different TV channels in her brain and that sometimes Gigi gets stuck on a negative channel that only has bad stuff to say. "I don't like school." "My friends don't like me." "I am too short compared to my friends." Ms. O has suggested that Gigi has other channels in her brain that she can "switch to" to feel more positive and hopeful, to interrupt all the bad stuff. This "positive channel" strategy also challenges Gigi's worries to show her that, in reality, her life is stable and good. It's a cool idea, right? This "channel" technique helps children take possession of their own minds and empowers them to make another choice about how they see the world. Changing their perspective can change their behavior! Classic CBT (cognitive behavioral therapy) move, and I loved it.

One night, Gigi came to me at bedtime and said, "Well, I really didn't want to go to bed because I wanted to read and play, and I started getting really mad and upset about it, but I switched my channel in my brain. I know that I need to go to bed and I switched into the part of my brain that knows this." Wow! Winner-winner, chicken dinner! Right? That channel technique worked right in front of my eyes. That means *it is a good technique for my child and should be effective forever and ever, amen.*

The very next morning, Gigi remembered she didn't do her homework. We had spent the previous day in religious celebrations and she simply forgot to do it. Not a big deal, or so I assumed. But because Gigi is sensitive and bright and cares deeply about what her teacher thinks of her (as many children do), she went into a spiral. "I cannot go to school. I am not ready. Everyone will think I'm lazy. Everyone will know I didn't do my work." I watched as her anxious tears began to slip down her cheeks, my own mind racing. But, oh, wait! The technique! "Gigi," I exclaimed, "let's change the channel! What would another channel say about the homework issue we are facing?"

Gigi stopped fretting and glared at me. "Mom, I am not doing that stupid channel thing."

Whoa, that went sideways! The amazingly perfect technique didn't work this time, but why?

Why was the wonderful technique now an utter failure? Should I never use it again? What had happened that, in one moment, my daughter embraced and used this channel technique and, in another moment, the technique had become a threat? Why do parenting techniques sometimes work and sometimes fail?

I'm guessing you've experienced this "success then failure" dynamic in your own parenting life. In my coaching career, I see this success/fail dynamic most frequently with the ubiquitous time-out. It goes like this: Parent gets sick of the three-year-old hitting. Parent complains about it at a play group or with neighbors. Parent is instructed to place the child on a step for about three minutes (one minute per age). Parent plunks the child on the step after hitting. Shocked child stays on the step, and the time-out works like a charm for a couple of days. By the fourth day, the child gets off the step, hits the parent, and runs away. The parent chases the child all over the house, threatening to make the child sit even longer. Said child hides under the bed, out of the parent's reach. Parent stomps away, irate, out of control, and confused. What changed? Why did the time-out work and then *stop* working?

Why do parenting techniques sometimes work and sometimes fail?

Another example is that the parent has purchased all of the Positive Parenting books and is now earnestly practicing emotion coaching with their children. This beautiful technique involves listening and validating your children's feelings with empathy, trying to help the child label the big feelings with words, set limits, *and* create solutions (think, "When you cannot play on the Xbox, that makes you feel angry and sad"). It is not an easy technique to master, but it is highly effective for many parents and their children. The emotion coaching is going pretty well, and then one day, the six-year-old literally screams in the parent's face, "STOP TALKING TO ME ABOUT MY FEELINGS AND LEAVE ME ALONE!" The child stomps away and slams their door, and the parent is left wondering what the heck happened. Why did the emotion coaching not work? It was such a perfect technique! The parent has been working so hard! What went wrong?

I have done a little noodling on why this dynamic occurs and created a little list of why even the best parenting techniques sometimes don't work or stop working:

- Maybe the parenting technique was never the right one to begin with, and you only had a one-off win at the start. This is particularly tough, because you can spend quite a bit of time pursuing a parenting technique before realizing it was never going to work, from the outset. For instance, you punish your ADHD eight-year-old son for not getting off his iPad when you ask. It works the first time because he is so shocked by the punishment, but then the punishment never works again. Why? Punishment plus executive-functioning issues most often equals more pushback from the child. I am not saying that there cannot be rules and consequences, but shaming and causing physical or emotional pain (punishment) almost never reinforces the behavior you want in an ADHD kiddo, hence that parenting strategy was doomed to fail from the get-go.

- I most frequently see the one-hit-wonder parent strategies when it comes to the dreaded time-out. Why? Well, most children are compliant (and shocked) enough to just sit on the step for a bit, the first time-out. But once the child's brain wakes up to the fact that we are plunking them on the step and leaving them there, the child becomes panicked (separation from our main attachment causes panic in all humans, but especially children), the child is off the step, is going to show you he is the boss of his body, and then the fighting is off to the races. There are some deep emotional impulses at work here, and whether you are locking children in rooms or putting them on steps, setting up that separation (both emotionally and physically) makes kids feel panicked and then sad. You don't think so? Have you ever had a friend or partner or lover ice you out during a fight? Refuse to speak to you? Ignore you? If you have, then you know how emotionally abusive and degrading it is. It follows that separating a young child from you to "teach them a lesson" is a parenting strategy that is likely to never work more than once or twice.*

- Another reason your technique may not be working is that you are not using the parenting technique consistently or in a manner that brings success. For instance, let's take the channel-changing idea for my sweet Gigi. Upon reflection, I had not used the technique on a daily basis, nor had I written the strategy down and posted it somewhere where we could both see it. I am hard-pressed to think of a child (any human, really) who doesn't need a visual reminder to help their brains in some small way, so Gigi probably needed me to practice this technique with some more

---

* You may have a child that took to time-outs beautifully. They worked wonders, and hence, you love time-outs. Great!

regularity. In order to give any parenting technique a fighting chance, you need to have a bit of a plan behind it, so shooting from the hip with any technique has a high chance of failure.

- Which brings me to the idea that you may not fully understand how or why the parenting technique is supposed to work to begin with. This happens *all the* time to parents, and it is mostly the result of reading too many parenting books. (Ironic? Yes, but I gotta tell it like I see it.) Here's the cycle: Shit is going down in your house. There are behavioral shenanigans all over the place, and your frustration is at an all-time high. In desperation, you buy or borrow the first book that is the most highly rated on Amazon (I know you do that because I have done that, too; I just bought a cookbook the same way), you skip the theory part of the parenting book and, instead, flip directly to the part of the book that tells you *what to do*. Without fully understanding the theory, the why, behind the parenting strategy or technique, you dive in with sticker charts or marble jars or breathing techniques or time-outs or emotion coaching or whatever else you are being told to do.

  And because you are applying the wrong bandage to the wrong wound, or a too large bandage to a small wound, or a teeny tiny Band-Aid to a gaping wound, the technique is destined to be a total failure. Not only does the technique fail, but your child's behavior is worse. You chuck the book in the trash or give it to the nearest Little Free Library, curse the author's name, and double down on punishments (because at least punishment feels like we are doing something and that feels good).

Again, this happens so often to the parents I work with that I'm shocked when I meet a parent who says, "Yup, I haven't read a blog or an article or a book. Haven't tried a thing." Instead, it is normal to have a problem and want to seek a solution, so I don't blame parents for trying (and failing) a myriad of techniques.

- You think the parenting strategy is meant to work forever, and it simply won't. Contracts and charts and apps and just about anything you can think of, they *all stop working*. This is not because the strategies are necessarily faulty; it is because kids grow and change so quickly. There is no failure here; it is just time doing its inevitable work. I most often see this dynamic around children's bedtime. The parents have lovingly developed a routine full of songs and sweetness, teeth brushing, and book choosing. And then, out of nowhere, the child is pushing you off. They want to brush their own teeth, they want to pick their own pajamas, and they don't want to play a game about picking books anymore. Your child is growing up and growing out of what used to work. A parent will call this misbehavior, but it is actually maturation and progress.

- Your heart isn't in the parenting technique from the start. Our hearts may not be fully in sync with certain parenting techniques for two reasons: (1) they don't jibe with our morals or fundamental ways of understanding the world, and/or (2) we haven't grieved the reality of letting something go to allow the technique to work. By way of an example, I have coached many parents who are desperately trying to sleep train a child on the heels of a health issue, a big transition, or simply a tough family situation. Thus, the heartache, anger, and parental fatigue is at an all-time high, and by the time they call me, they are desperate to get their child into their own bed. By listening to their stories, it becomes apparent that there is nothing wrong with the sleep-training methods they're employing: The parents are using the encouraging words, they are connecting to their sweet (and exhausted) child, and they aren't threatening or punishing the child for hopping out of bed. All the boxes are checked when it comes to doing "the right thing." So, what is missing? The parent's heart isn't in it. The parent is also giving up and giving in because they are so darn tired. For a million reasons, the parent cannot sustain the patience and willpower to keep up the strategy to keep the child in their own bed. Like the single mother who teaches all day, grades all night, and has a two-year-old who is desperately needy for Mom's smell and touch. Yes, the mom wants the child in her own "big girl bed," but the mom is simply too exhausted to keep putting her back in while she shrieks. Her heart isn't in it, and she gives up.

Or I have coached parents where one parent is working twelve-hour days while the other parent cares for their parent in hospice. The emotional toll of watching their parent slip away means that the sleep training has fallen to the side, and the five-year-old climbs into her parents' bed every night. The parents are too overwhelmed to take on the training; their hearts aren't in it. And I have often coached the parents who believe that their children *should* be sleeping with them at night, but their pediatrician, mother, and neighbor have guilted and shamed them into sleep training, only for the parent to give up every effective sleep-training method as soon as the child whines once. The parent doesn't believe in what they are doing; the method is not going to work. Repeat this idea (the parent's heart not being in the methods) around toilet training, homework, activities, and chores, as well as holding boundaries, and you can see the problem.

• Sometimes your strategies don't work because you are trying to swap out good old-fashioned boundary-holding for a well-intentioned (but wishy-washy) strategy. If I had a nickel for every time a parent needed to tell their children one good firm "NO," but instead they try emotion coaching and empathic listening and meditative breathing techniques and so on and so forth, I would have a lot of money. Many parents (I count myself here) want a strategy to sidestep the hard parts of parenting, and that is never going to happen. Even while you use every trick in the book, you still need to hold good old-fashioned boundaries with your children.

• Finally, the reason that fancy parenting strategies and techniques often don't work is because parents forget that the most powerful parenting tool is always available to them: the power of their own attachment to their children. It isn't exciting and it isn't as immediately satisfying as, say, a punishment, but humans are built to connect. Children are built to stay in their parents' orbit, children are built to grow and mature in their parents' compassionate presence, and lastly, children make it through the hardships of life with their parents at their side. It all may sound a little pie in the sky, but I have yet to coach parents whereby, softening their hearts, they don't find a way to connect and relax with their children. The parents remember to have fun, smile, and bring some joy to the day-to-day grind. And while it seems obvious, if your connection with your children isn't in good working order, your techniques will be harder to implement. Children who don't feel connected to their parents aren't interested in being cooperative and easy.

After all of this consideration of parenting strategies, I want you to remember this: When a parenting strategy isn't working, step back and give it some space. Don't push. No one is failing; there is no need to fret. Step back and reflect on the above thoughts.

REFLECT AND WRITE

1. If you review the above list of why your parenting strategies may not be working, what sticks out to you?

2. Do you feel too reliant on strategies, tricks, and tips to try to get your kids to behave?

3.   Do you trust your connection with your children to carry you through some rough times?

4.   Are you okay with letting some of your strategies go to see what happens? What are your biggest fears?

5.   Do you believe that you can trust yourself to do what works for your family?

CHAPTER 14

The Invisible Work of Parenting

Things You Didn't Put on Your Résumé
by Joyce Sutphen

How often you got up in the middle of the night
when one of your children had a bad dream,
and sometimes you woke because you thought
you heard a cry but they were all sleeping,
so you stood in the moonlight just listening
to their breathing, and you didn't mention
that you were an expert at putting toothpaste
on tiny toothbrushes and bending down to wiggle
the toothbrush ten times on each tooth while
you sang the words to songs from *Annie*, and
who would suspect that you know the fingerings
to the songs in the first four books of the Suzuki
Violin Method and that you can do the voices

of Pooh and Piglet especially well, though
your absolute favorite thing to read out loud is
Bedtime for Frances and that you picked
up your way of reading it from Glynis Johns,
and it is, now that you think of it, rather impressive
that you read all of Narnia and all of the Ring Trilogy
(and others too many to mention here) to them
before they went to bed and on the way out to
Yellowstone, which is another thing you don't put
on the résumé: how you took them to the ocean
and the mountains and brought them safely home.

I could not breastfeed my first child for the first couple weeks of her life She could barely take a bottle. She simply would not latch on to my breast. She was too little and too tired, and I was too engorged and too needy. I don't blame myself, but I know my body vibrated with insecurity and panic, and how was she expected to latch on to *that*? My body beat with a steady drum: "She's starving, she's starving, she's starving . . ."

I would sit in the glider, at all hours of the night, holding my tiny baby upright, trying to keep any modicum of breastmilk in her belly. If I close my eyes, I can still see the ice glistening on the bare branches of the redbud tree outside the window, and I can hear the late January wind howling. There would be a miracle hour, here and there, where she would eat a little and snuggle into me and I could feel my body begin to unwind; my heart would unclench and I would almost rest. I wouldn't cry at the ache in my swollen breasts and I didn't call to my spouse to come help; I just rocked and stared at the ice and listened to the wind. I was determined to sit there, hold her upright, and use my sheer willpower to make her gain weight.

No one saw these moments. Not my husband, snoring. Not my

parents, who stayed with me to help. No one. These attempts to feed her, as well as my determination to not weep on top of her, are like most of our parenting moments that matter: They were utterly invisible to the whole world.

When I coach parents these days, I talk often about our invisible parenting work. When a father is shuffling the three-year-old and the baby into the car and *doesn't* lose his patience, when the mother *doesn't* sigh loudly after the five-year-old breaks eggshells into the batter, when the parent stays quiet when she sees pee in the underwear *again*, when the mom walks away from the sassy tween without her own sharp retort, when the dad listens (without commentary) as his daughter blows off steam about the soccer coach, when the parent doesn't drag the child to their room, when the parent silently hugs the child crying about homework, when the parent doesn't lecture about the mean friends . . . and on and on it goes. No one sees any of these small decisions. And while there are parenting columns, blogs, books, and lists chock-full of "what to do when," there is even greater power in these unseen moments.

Several times a year, I travel to my Buddhist sangha where we sit in silence for about four days. Before you get any wacky ideas about what we are doing, allow me to clarify: All we do is sit, eat, sleep, walk, and repeat. There is nothing transcendental or mysterious or layered about it. I sit in silence for the sheer purpose of sitting in silence. Sometimes, at the start of a retreat, I wonder to myself, *What the hell am I doing here? I have so much important stuff to do!* And then my teacher always says something like this: "You may wonder how sitting in silence could be of any use to you. You may wonder why you have made this effort; who you are possibly helping by sitting here, doing nothing, while the world is on fire? Well, by sitting here, in silence, you are hurting no one. You are causing no harm to your family, your coworkers, yourself." When I hear this, I often exhale and become teary, because I know how much damage I can do to people I love. I know I can be angry and petty and frustrated. I know I can hurt my children with just my energy; I can make them insecure and on edge.

This is the power of *doing no harm*; the power of doing the good parenting work, unseen. The power of trusting that your efforts are worth something simply because, well, you did them. We don't know what will become of all these little unseen and peaceful moments, but that's not our immediate concern. You are parenting this way because it is your role to keep showing up. This is not a provocative idea, the idea of thinking of how much harm you *haven't* caused to your children and family. America is a country of doers, of work made manifest, a culture of tangible results. We don't want to wait; we want outcomes now, now, now. If I am kind to my child, I want her to be grateful *now*. If I demonstrate sharing with my child, I want her to share *now*. If I serve food to my child, I want her to eat it and like it *now*. If I hug my child, I want her to hug me back *now*. Because we sometimes misunderstand parenting as an immediate "if A then B" proposition, we cannot see the positive and long-term results of small and unseen parenting moments. We don't know the good in making the lunch, smoothing the hair, reading one more chapter, changing the soiled underwear, listening to the whining about a classmate, missing the work meeting for the morning school share, carpooling to the practice, picking up from the school dance at 11:00 p.m., finding the socks and shin guards, and blowing on the hot soup. While we all wait for the immediate thank-yous, we don't see the invisible threads that we are weaving together to create the net of love for our children to fall into much, much later.

I don't want to blow smoke; some of us (me) need real parenting goals and we need to work toward them. The very essence of the coaching work I do is the creation of parenting homework and goals. The brain loves a direction, and it is appropriate and kind to give our brains somewhere to go, a task. So then, how do we balance this desire to make real changes in our parenting lives with the need to slow down and stop doing, doing, doing? How can we pause to recognize that we already are doing the important work of parenting, even without all of the showy examples that are out there in the world (thank you, Insta)? How do we appreciate the unseen moments of peace while aspiring to do, frankly, better?

The Power of Showing Up

To begin this attempt at balance, let's accept that showing up for our kids, day in and day out, is a real accomplishment. Maybe my standards are too low or maybe I have been working too long, but I have seen a fair number of parents who don't show up for their children, both physically and emotionally. Whether the neglect was due to addiction or untreated mental illness or overwork or the distraction of messy marriages, there are plenty of parents who do not see their children, smile at them, or even embrace them on a daily basis. These parents may hold too many or not enough boundaries, and they cannot even discern if the boundaries are helping or hurting their children. These parents are not "good" or "bad," and putting them into boxes would be too easy. From generational neglect to poverty to illness to systemic cultural issues, I understand how this happens. I understand how parents disconnect from their children, and I understand that some parents' needs and neediness are simply too great to bridge the gap to their children. Just scratching the surface of these parents will often reveal deep struggles and pain. This isn't a pass for abusive behavior or stubbornness; this is simply the reality of being a human. Nothing is ever black and white.

Maybe you had a childhood like this, where your basic needs were mostly met, but your parents were cold, unavailable, or simply not able to love you in the way that you needed to be loved. Maybe you grew up in a home where you were smothered; your parents hovered and kept you in an endless state of anxiety as they awaited your next move. Or maybe you grew up in the elusive but existent "perfect" home. Your parents loved you *just right*. In any case, if you *mostly* awaken and smile at your child today, embrace them, hold them when they cry, celebrate them when they win, listen to their stories, eat with them, read to them, challenge them, hold the necessary boundaries, allow the anger and tears, then *you are fully parenting*. Even if you are doing this, like, 70 percent of the time? Winning! And if you hold your tongue at the eye roll, decide to not care what they wear to school, and allow them to fail without chronic hand-wringing? Well, that's icing on the cake.

American parenting has become so intense, so theory-driven, so bullet-listed, neuroscience-y, data-driven, technique-heavy, and expert-laden that simply believing you are doing "good enough" by lovingly showing up is a rebellious act. No one asks, "How did you *not* decimate your child's confidence today?" or "So, how did you not lose your patience when your four-year-old cried for twenty minutes about the TV?" No. Our culture repeatedly asks what we put *into* our children, like if we don't constantly fill them up, they will disappear into thin air.

"Bully-Proofing Kids!"

"Completely Preventing Addiction of Every Type"

"Stopping Anxiety in Its Tracks"

"Creating Readers"

"Expanding Your Child's Palate"

"Bring Out Your Child's Inner Artist"

The options are endless and there is nothing wrong with any of these topics. But how can a parent do *all* of this? How can we keep a home, make money, and keep adding to our children's lives in this à la carte fashion? No matter what you do, it is never enough. And the worst part? We don't understand the power that we already have. The power to keep simply showing up.

So, instead of going down the rabbit hole of "never enough," why don't we actively remember the simple parenting moments, the moments that we chose peace, bravery, and compassion over anger, fear, and hard-heartedness? For instance, when I turned my head for one second and lost my child on the beach when she was two, and I almost lost my mind with panic and fear. (And she was found, safe and sound, by an elderly man two lifeguard stands down.) I could have gone haywire for years, I could have decided that she could never leave my sight ever again, and I needed to homeschool her in my basement forever and ever, but instead I chose to feel confident in my ability to not lose her as well as her ability to stay with me. Another example? I could focus on the first time one of my kids screamed "shut the fuck up" in my face as an epic parenting fail, or I could focus on the fact that I didn't smack her face when she did it. Or! I could focus on the teacher's email detailing how disruptive my child was in class, or I could focus on how gently and firmly I handled it, leaving us with a doable plan instead of overreactive shaming.

Given that anxiety is rampant in our lives (never higher) and that most of us are inundated with statistics that make our blood run cold, it's no wonder that we are quick to see our parenting faults and failures. Parents call me daily with a litany of woes: They aren't sensitive enough to their children, they aren't patient enough, they are making their children anxious with their own anxiety, they don't understand their children, and sometimes, the parents just don't like their own kids. But after I ask the parent to list everything great about their children (and these lists are always long), the parents have to face a hard truth: If we are going to take responsibility for everything hard about our children, then we should take responsibility for everything good about them, too. This reality forces the parent to take a beat. "Could it be," I ask, "that your child is sometimes difficult and it has nothing to do with you? Could it be, as well, that your child is awesome, and that also has nothing to do with you?"

How can this be?

Your Child Is Not a Product

On one hand, this child is completely and utterly himself. When sperm met egg, that moment contained all the potentiality of your child, a true miracle. But then the parent and the environment have an undeniably major impact on the child's physical and mental health, as well as the trajectory of their lives. This dichotomy of "let your child become who they are" mixed with "everything you do with and to your child creates a lasting imprint" is so mind-blowingly big that usually our parent brain settles on, *Well, I am doing this all wrong.* Our brains are set on a channel to keep us protective and nervous and watchful; you aren't crazy. So, if you want to find what you did wrong (I couldn't breastfeed my baby), that will be simple work for you. Your brain will happily comply. But if you want to pivot to how you did something peaceful or didn't make something *worse* (I eventually gave up that horrific breastfeeding), the pivot is available to you. This pivot, though, requires some serious mindfulness.

In some (not all) of the Mindful and Positive Parenting literature, it can feel like you are only meant to attune to your child. "How is he feeling? What is she thinking? Why did he just react like that? Why did she say that to me?" I mean, you can begin to feel full-tilt paranoid and begin just watching your child rather than *parenting them*, but if you turn that mindfulness to yourself, you can begin to focus on the only person you can actually control in this life: you. You can see your feelings, thoughts, reactions, and behaviors as part of the elaborate dance with your child, and if you do this enough, you will see a pattern emerge: Yes, you do make parenting mistakes galore, but your child is also their own person with their own peccadilloes and eccentricities. You are *not* the sole mover of every part of your child; you cannot own it all.

It wasn't my fault my baby was too small to eat.

It wasn't even my fault that I lost my two-year-old on the beach.

It isn't your fault that your child has ADHD.

It isn't your fault that your child is intense.

It isn't your fault that your child is dyslexic.

It is just life being all . . . life-y.

And the only thing we can control is our reaction to life being the way it truly is. This is a hard pill, but one that's worthwhile to swallow if you want to keep your head above the parenting waves.

So yes, you have made parenting mistakes, both huge and small. Yes, you probably have some apologies to make (see Chapter 12), but when you kick off your shoes, put down your bag, and flop on the couch to hug the child you haven't seen all day, *that's parenting*, my friend. When you heat up the leftovers or serve the cold pizza, and you smile at your child? That's parenting, too. When you stay up late in bed, reading a book about ADHD or SPD or autism or giftedness or allergies or 504s and IEPs, that's good parenting. Because our culture is only focused on the outcomes of what we *do*, we forget the good that comes from the trying, too. We forget the good that comes from simplicity and peace. And because no one will praise you for the damage you haven't caused, let me go ahead and do that for you. Well done, you!

Now, here are you: You've just read a book, chock-full of advice-like parenting notions. Am I now suggesting that you chuck it all and just sit back with your good intentions? No. I just want you to *include* all these little moments when you decide that you suck as a parent. Instead of kitchen-sinking your entire existence, let's *mindfully* take stock of all of the caretaking you do. These little parenting moments count, they matter, and they should be recognized. If you are going to beat yourself up for your crappy meals or raised voices, you also have to congratulate yourself for the laughter, the wins, and the joy.

REFLECT AND WRITE

1. Do you believe that you have a profound impact on your child, but that your job is also to get out of your child's way? Can you accept this contradictory element of parenting?

2. Make a brief list of how and why your child is awesome. Only you will see this list, so have at it. Reflect on this list and ask yourself: Which traits did you insert into your child and which did you help grow or help emerge?

3. Do you think that blaming yourself for everything wrong with your child is kind of egotistical? (And yes, I am suggesting it may be.)

4. Every night, write down or share with a partner or a friend how you didn't make something worse. Share how you stayed in control or peaceful or kind or kept a tough boundary. Share that it was tiring and no one saw it, but it was worth it. It was your invisible and meaningful parenting work.

Easier Said Than Done

Anything worth doing in this life is easier said than done. Forcing yourself to bed earlier (while leaving your smartphone in another room) is easier said than done. Taking the stairs to promote heart health, when the elevator is right there, is easier said than done. Seeing the doctor about that weird mole you've been watching grow? Easier said than done. Opening the bills and truly looking at your debt is definitely easier said than done.

I have never once done anything in my life (that actually mattered) where it wasn't easier to say it than do it. It is easy to be lazy. It is easy to spend money and eat junk and be mean and use up resources and *not* ask how people are doing. It is easy to love someone and not tell them, as well as stay angry and simmer in silence. It is easy to carry resentments and blame others, to behave badly and ignore your big emotions.

So, I want to end this book by letting you know that, with some urgency, I want you to *act* in your parenting life. James Clear, author of *Atomic Habits*, says:

> How long does it take to build a habit? Twenty-one days?
> Thirty days? Sixty-six days? The honest answer is: forever.
> Because once you stop doing it, it is no longer a habit. A
> habit is a lifestyle to be lived, not a finish line to be crossed.
> Make small, sustainable changes you can stick with.

My sincerest hope is that, after reading this book, you now have a journal or a document full of parenting ideas, things that struck you as important or trivial or smart or disappointing. All ideas, good or bad, are pie in the sky until you take action. So, please, choose something from your ideas about your parenting life and do it, and here is the most important bit: Just see what happens. I was recently listening to a podcast by Kate Swoboda about the commitment to excellence, and she said something that stuck with me (I am paraphrasing here): "Any step toward deep personal work yields rewards. It may not be the rewards you thought they would be, but deep work is never wasted." I was on a long walk when I heard this, and I thought about this commitment to excellence for a couple of miles, how parenting is a roller coaster of deep, personal work and it certainly yields many results, most of them you never dreamed of. And yet, as long as you work toward intentional change, *something* will happen.

When it comes to diving into deeper parenting waters, as well as breaking out of all the parenting theories and rules, it isn't enough to just start a new strategy and poof! That's it; everything is changed. This isn't about drinking more water for your health (which I also always recommend); this may be about increasing your connection with your child or taking responsibility for too many boundaries or not enough boundaries. It may be about addressing your controlling ways or maybe how you are afraid of your child. Remember: You are interacting with another complex human; therefore, it is going to be complicated. The idea of your effort equaling the change in your mind simply isn't realistic. Just don't give up. Every effort in a positive direction is worth it, even if you don't see the results right away.

> ## Every effort in a positive direction is worth it.

Maybe you have a journal of huge ideas, maybe you have one thing to focus on. In either case, here are some thoughts for how to move forward with your best parenting intentions (again, remembering that all is easier said than done):

- Find your people. (Trust me, you *know* when you aren't with your people.)

- Find a therapist or coach to keep you honest.

- Share your goals with a friend who keeps you honest.

- Figure out why boundaries with your children are so damn hard.

- Figure out why you are a control freak.

- Decide to stop working on your partner and stick to improving yourself.

- Be less busy.

- Get busier.

- Make your intentions an alert in your phone. (My current alert says, "What is my lane here?")

- Find good resources to learn about child development.

- Sign up for parenting classes.

- Stop learning about parenting and just listen to your intuition.

- Praise other parents and mean it. (It is funny how this makes you a better parent, like, immediately.)

- Take a break from your million parenting techniques and focus on one thing. (Check out Rick Hanson for more ideas on focusing on one thing.)

- Expect better from yourself.

- Expect less from yourself.

You see that many things on this list are paradoxical, because it all depends on what you and your children need. It is okay; don't overthink it. Just act. Remember, you are not beholden to any one theory or strategy! You know your child best, you know your family best, and you know yourself best. The experts and books will only help you if you courageously break out of the rules our culture places on us and take a chance.

Thanks for reading, and good luck. ;)

RECOMMENDED READING

Ames, Louise Bates, Ph.D. *Your One-Year-Old* (and series)

Aron, Elaine N., Ph.D. *The Highly Sensitive Child*

Bowlby, John. *A Secure Base*

Boyce, W. Thomas, M.D. *The Orchid and the Dandelion*

Bronson, Po. *NurtureShock*

Brown, Brené. *Daring Greatly*

Cain, Susan. *Quiet: The Power of Introverts in a World That Can't Stop Talking*

Chapman, Gary. *The 5 Love Languages of Children*

Chödrön, Pema. *Fail, Fail Again, Fail Better*

Clear, James. *Atomic Habits*

Dell'Antonia, KJ. *How to Be a Happier Parent*

Duffy, Dr. John. *Parenting the New Teen in the Age of Anxiety*

Eanes, Rebecca. *Positive Parenting*

Fagell, Phyllis L. *Middle School Matters*

Fass, Paula S. *The End of American Childhood*

Fey, Tina. *Bossypants*

Foldes, Katherine. *Family Meeting Workbook*

Fonseca, Christine. *Emotional Intensity in Gifted Students*

Frank, Hillary. *Weird Parenting Wins*

Galinsky, Ellen. *Mind in the Making*

Gopnik, Alison. *The Gardener and the Carpenter*

Greene, Ross W., Ph.D. *The Explosive Child*

———. *Raising Human Beings*

Hanson, Rick, Ph.D. *Buddha's Brain*

Kabat-Zinn, Myla and Jon. *Everyday Blessings*

Karen, Robert, Ph.D. *Becoming Attached*

Kenison, Katrina. *The Gift of an Ordinary Day*

———. *Mitten Strings for God*

Kindlon, Dan, Ph.D., and Michael Thompson, Ph.D. *Raising Cain*

Kohn, Alfie. *Unconditional Parenting*

Kranowitz, Carol Stock. *The Out-of-Sync Child*

Lahey, Jessica. *The Gift of Failure*

Lansbury, Janet. *No Bad Kids*

Lerner, Harriet, Ph.D. *The Dance of Anger*

Lewis, Katherine Reynolds. *The Good News About Bad Behavior*

Lythcott-Haims, Julie. *How to Raise an Adult*

MacNamara, Deborah, Ph.D. *Rest, Play, Grow*

Madaras, Lynda and Area. *My Body, My Self*

Markham, Dr. Laura. *Peaceful Parent, Happy Kids*

———. *Peaceful Parent, Happy Siblings*

Martin, William. *The Parent's Tao Te Ching*

Maté, Gabor. *Scattered Minds*

Miller, Alice. *The Drama of the Gifted Child*

Miller, Karen Maezen. *Hand Wash Cold*

———. *Momma Zen*

———. *Paradise in Plain Sight*

Miner, Julianna. *Raising a Screen-Smart Kid*

Natterson, Cara. *Decoding Boys*

Naumburg, Carla, Ph.D. *How to Stop Losing Your Sh*t with Your Kids*

Nepo, Mark. *The Book of Awakening*

Neufeld, Gordon, Ph.D., and Gabor Maté, M.D. *Hold On to Your Kids*

Obama, Michelle. *Becoming*

O'Sullivan, John. *Changing the Game*

Payne, Kim John. *Simplicity Parenting*

Pearsall, Paul, Ph.D. *The Heart's Code*

Pink, Daniel H. *Drive*

Rapp, Doris, M.D. *Is This Your Child?*

Reber, Deborah. *Differently Wired*

Reichert, Michael C. *How to Raise a Boy*

Roffman, Deborah M. *Sex and Sensibility: The Thinking Parent's Guide to Talking Sense About Sex*

Rosenthal, Norman E. *The Gift of Adversity*

Samudio, Mercedes. *Shame-Proof Parenting*

Sax, Leonard, M.D. *The Collapse of Parenting*

Schaefer, Dr. Charles E., and Theresa Foy DiGeronimo. *Ages and Stages: A Parent's Guide to Normal Childhood Development*

Siegel, Daniel J., M.D. *Brainstorm*

———*The Mindful Brain*

———*Mindsight*

———*Parenting from the Inside Out*

Siegel, Daniel J., M.D., and Tina Payne Bryson, Ph.D. *No Drama Discipline*

————. *The Whole-Brain Child*

Silverberg, Cory. *Sex Is a Funny Word*

Simmons, Rachel. *Odd Girl Out*

Stiffelman, Susan. *Parenting with Presence*

Stixrud, William, Ph.D., and Ned Johnson. *The Self-Driven Child*

Swingle, Mari K., Ph.D. *i-Minds*

Trudeau, Renée Peterson. *The Mother's Guide to Self-Renewal*

————. *Nurturing the Soul of Your Family*

Tsabary, Shefali, Ph.D. *The Awakened Family*

van der Kolk, Bessel, M.D. *The Body Keeps the Score*

Webb, James T., Janet L. Gore, Edward R. Amend, and Arlene R. DeVries. *A Parent's Guide to Gifted Children*

Zucker, Bonnie. *Anxiety-Free Kids*

ACKNOWLEDGMENTS

This book may have my name on it, but there are many people who helped birth it.

First, thank you to every parent with whom I've worked, who has read my work, and who I've met on the street or spoken with on the phone. You continue to challenge and inspire me to be a better coach, writer, parent, and woman and for that? I am forever grateful.

To my parents, Hugh Jr. and Kathleen Leahy: Your endless support and encouragement keeps me going. I wasn't the easiest to raise, but you stuck with me. Thank you and I love you. To my brother, Hugh Leahy III: Thanks for allowing me to use you as an example in my writings. To my aunt Liz Slater: Thank you for loving me unconditionally when I needed it most. Thanks to the Rasevic and Leahy clans for patiently listening to me repeat, "I gotta go work on my book," for what must have felt like a hundred years. To Jen Middleton, Ashley Bekton, Pleasance Silicki, Tim and Lauren Angeloni, and Peggy Seas for asking about the book and pondering the most (and least) important aspects of it; I love you all. To Gwen Castleberry, who keeps MLPC going, keeps me sane, and believes in me, no matter what. Everything is going to be *fine*, Gwen.

To Marian Lizzi, editor in chief at TarcherPerigee: Your compassion, kindness, humor, insights, and belief in me made this process so much better than I could have ever imagined. To my editor, Gail

Ross: I am so grateful for your guidance and kindness; I know I can be a handful, so thank you for hanging in there.

To Amy Joyce, the editor of On Parenting at the *Washington Post*: What can I say? I owe so much to you; I am forever grateful. Your keen eye, kind critiques, and clear voice have left an indelible mark on this book and me, and any good writing I do is in large part, due to you. I love you to pieces.

To Dr. Gordon Neufeld, all the faculty at the Neufeld Institute, and especially Darlene Denis-Friske: Thank you for opening my eyes and giving language to the basic truths that every parent needs and wants. Without all of you, I would not have been able to write this book.

To Karen Maezen Miller, the Dewdrop Sangha, and the Hazy Moon Sangha: Thank you for the continuous encouragement in my ongoing efforts to sit and be quiet (and what an effort it is).

Thank you to everyone and everything who ever encouraged me to keep going, in life and in parenting. Every professor at the Catholic University and Johns Hopkins University, and every parent and teacher at PEP and the schools in which I have worked. Thank you to Wilmington, Delaware, for toughening me up and Lewes, Delaware, for softening me. Finally, thank you to my writing partner, Ollie, for the walks, cuddles, and naps.

Meghan Leahy is the mother of three daughters. She practices Zen Buddhism, holds a bachelor's degree in English and secondary education and a master's degree in school counseling, and she is a certified parent coach and Neufeld Institute Facilitator, as well as the On Parenting columnist at the *Washington Post*. Leahy lives with her family outside Washington, DC.